JAMIE MAXWELL is an Edinburgh-based politi[cal journalist who writes] for the *New Statesman* and *Bella Caledon[ia, as well as the]* *Sunday Herald*, the *Scottish Review of Books*, the *Scotsman* and the *Sunday Mail*. Last year he edited *The Case for Left Wing Nationalism*, a collection of his late father Stephen Maxwell's essays. He is the co-author (with David Torrance) of *Scotland's Referendum: A Guide for Voters* and is currently co-editing, with Pete Ramand, *Old Nations, Auld Enemies, New Times*, the selected essays of Tom Nairn.

OWEN DUDLEY EDWARDS FRSE is Hon. Fellow of the School of History, Classics and Archaeology, at the University of Edinburgh where he taught History from 1968, having been born in Ireland and studied in the USA. His wife Bonnie is American and his three children are Scots. His most recent major monograph is *British Children's Fiction in the Second World War*, his most recent collaboration *Tartan Pimps*, and he has edited several books including *A Claim of Right for Scotland*.

DUNCAN MacLAREN is an Adjunct Professor of the Australian Catholic University where he lectured in international development studies and ethics. He was Executive Director of SCIAF, the aid agency of the Scottish Catholic Church, and Secretary General of Caritas, one of the largest aid and development networks in the world. He is a lay Dominican.

JEANE FREEMAN OBE is a political analyst, chair of the Golden Jubilee National Hospital and a member if the Judicial Appointments Board for Scotland. Having served as senior political advisor to First Minister Jack McConnell in 2002 to 2005, she is now a leading figure in Women for Independence.

JAMES FOLEY is the author of *Yes: The Radical Case for Scottish Independence*. He is finishing his PhD on the Scottish economy at the University of Edinburgh and he lectures at Napier University.

ROBIN MCALPINE is the director of the Jimmy Reid Foundation, a member of the Common Weal and the editor of the *Scottish Left Review*. Having graduated from Glasgow University, he became Press Officer to George Robertson, then Shadow Secretary of State for Scotland and leader of the Scottish Labour Party. Returning to Scotland to work in policy development, Robin was also Public Affairs Manager for Universities Scotland for eight years. He is now one of the most well-known and influential voices for independence and social renewal in Scotland.

CAT BOYD is a leading Scottish trade union activist. She is co-founder of and campaigns for the Radical Independence Campaign and People's Assembly Scotland. She is also a founder and Chair of Coalition of Resistance Scotland, and has previously held the position of PCS Young Members Officer. She has appeared as a speaker at the Radical Independence Conference 2013. Recently, she collaborated with Jenny Morrison on a manifesto entitled *Women and Scottish Independence: A Feminist Response.*

BOB THOMSON worked as engineering draughtsman, then as trade union official, retiring as Associate Scottish Secretary, UNISON. He is a former member of the General Council of the STUC. A Labour Party member for over 50 years and a past Chairman and Treasurer of the Scottish Labour Party, he served as a lay member of employment tribunals and the Employment Appeal Tribunal. Active in human rights organisations in the UK and Scotland including Scottish Human Rights Trust, he is currently Convener of the Jimmy Reid Foundation, a think tank and advocacy group, who have commissioned the Common Weal Papers which detail a blueprint for a fairer, more equal, more productive society in an independent or devolved Scotland.

Luath Press is an independently owned and managed book publishing company based in Scotland, and is not aligned to any political party or grouping. *Viewpoints* is an occasional series exploring issues of current and future relevance.

Why Not?

Scotland, Labour and Independence

Edited by
JAMIE MAXWELL and OWEN DUDLEY EDWARDS

Luath Press Limited
EDINBURGH
www.luath.co.uk

First published 2014

ISBN: 978-1-910021-19-4

The paper used in this book is recyclable. It is made from
low chlorine pulps produced in a low energy, low emissions manner
from renewable forests.

Printed and bound by
Bell & Bain Ltd., Glasgow

Typeset in 11 point Sabon
by 3btype.com

The authors' right to be identified as author of this work under the
Copyright, Designs and Patents Act 1988 has been asserted.

© the contributors

To the memory of Michael Foot.

And of

Bob McLean

Contents

Acknowledgements		9
Introduction		11
CHAPTER ONE	Realising Labour Values *Jeane Freeman*	21
CHAPTER TWO	War and Peace *Owen Dudley Edwards*	27
CHAPTER THREE	Britain, Global Development and Scotland *Duncan MacLaren*	45
CHAPTER FOUR	Backlash: The Political Economy of Voting NO *James Foley*	53
CHAPTER FIVE	The Meaning of Things *Robin McAlpine*	61
CHAPTER SIX	Ireland: The Real Elephant in the Room *Owen Dudley Edwards*	68
CHAPTER SEVEN	Thank you, Edwin Morgan, Thank you, J.K. Rowling *Owen Dudley Edwards*	83
CHAPTER EIGHT	Putting the Past to Work for the Future *Jamie Maxwell*	100
CHAPTER NINE	To Win Scotland for its People *Cat Boyd*	106
CHAPTER TEN	On Not Standing Still *Bob Thomson*	112

Acknowledgements

Our deepest thanks are due to the National Library of Scotland, for their lovely café where this book was hatched, and especially to Gavin MacDougall of Luath, and his team, for services far beyond the norm. It is a privilege to work with them.

Introduction

THE BOOK TO READ ON Scottish Independence is Stephen Maxwell's *Arguing for Independence*. We edited it for publication by Luath Press after the author's death. He was Jamie's father and Owen's friend. We are still deeply conscious of how much we need him and our biggest criticism of the present book is that it doesn't have his living guidance.

As we enter on the last weeks before the Referendum on Independence we are particularly conscious of the need to win YES votes from many people who don't believe in Scottish nationalism and fear that voting YES would betray their allegiance to the Labour party or their belief that voting is a waste of time or some other reason, but who share all or most of the ideals and beliefs of YES voters. What is written here are things to think about. The Referendum is a means of fulfilling what many Scots want to happen although they have not all realised it.

In particular we think of the great back-breaking work carried out for so long by our fellow Socialists from its foundation and long before. YES is in the tradition of Robert Burns and Thomas Muir, Robert Owen and Hugh Miller, Robert Bontine Cunninghame Graham and James Connolly, John MacLean and James Maxton, Keir Hardie and Tom Johnston, John Wheatley and John McGovern, Hugh MacDiarmid and Somhairle MacGillcain, Hamish Henderson and John McGrath, Margo MacDonald and Anthony Ross, David Daiches and Lionel Daiches, Norman MacCaig and David MacLennan. Some lived too early to be in the Independent Labour Party or the Labour Party itself. Some were proud and great members of the Labour Party, some were never in it, some were intermittently in it. All were Socialists but not all gave themselves that label. Some were not for Scottish Independence in their time but what they thought, said and did helped to make those who vote YES on September 18.

And we do not claim the cause of Scottish Independence as purely Socialist. We do claim that it is the best and surest way of Scotland becoming Socialist. To put it in obvious maths, independent Scotland will be prevented by international law from having weapons of mass destruction since no country that has not had them is permitted to have them.

Thousands died in Iraq because of the belief it had such weapons, although, it did not. It is horribly evident that all the Unionist parties at Westminster are determined to retain them, much as an alcoholic hangs on to his bottle despite all medical and moral evidence. If weapons of mass destruction are outlawed in Scotland, there will be much difficulty about putting them anywhere else and so the day may dawn when the fact may sink in that not only are they destructive, debasing and damnable, but they are more trouble than they are worth. And if we get their blood-money off our books, we will have the funds to maintain the welfare state for which Labour fought so hard and so well in times past. Above all we will be able to maintain the National Health won and begun by Aneurin Bevan, and ensure continued investment in education to reach the widest possible number as his wife, the Scottish Socialist Jennie Lee, sought in her great stewardship of the Open University now starved of the funds it needs.

But we also claim inheritance of another tradition, all the more in dedicating this book to the memory of Michael Foot, a friend of Owen's for many years. Michael was a pioneer in the Aldermaston March in opposition to the ownership of nuclear weapons. He was a magnificent custodian of the Socialist tradition of these islands, and was proud that his name was given him partly in honour of the Irish nationalist and socialist, Michael Davitt, father of the Irish Land League and inspirer of the Scottish crofters' revolt and the early Scottish Labour movement. Michael Foot had a genius for finding the value of ideas held by historical figures few would associate with Socialism. His literary masterpiece *The Pen and the Sword* (1958) described and explained Swift's destruction of The Warlord Marlborough from his own knowledge of political journalism above all as editor of *Tribune*, but he showed how profoundly Swift hated war, ridiculed and condemned it and passionately denounced the whole cult of it. He took up the cause of devolution not in some would-be Machiavellian spirit of frustrating political rivals, but because he believed that in both Scotland and Wales nationalism showed some qualities meriting respect, and winning allegiance for genuinely altruistic reasons. He saw that love of community fuelled nationalism and socialism. He loved the Labour movement but never saw politics as a battle-field to gain jobs for the boys and power for the greedy. He fought to win devolution for Scotland, regardless of being misunderstood by those outside the Labour party, and being betrayed by some of those in it. He had a splendid sense of humour, and was one of the kindest men Owen has ever known.

He was very proud of partnership with John Smith, whose integrity, wisdom and laughter were a great counterpart to Michael's. We don't claim either of them as YES men, since all that can be known about how the dead would feel about now is that they would feel dead, though it is impossible to think of two who were so splendidly alive, as dead. They had a breadth of mind, a readiness to reconsider views to which they had been opposed, a love of humanity shown in friendships with people of goodwill for beyond party bounds. Michael fought to gain a Welsh language TV when Gwynfor Evans threatened to die on hunger-strike if Thatcher continued to reject one, and in fact his intervention carried the day with the aid of William Whitelaw, and Gwynfor survived. John Smith was piped to his grave in Iona by his lifelong friend Neil MacCormick MEP, the greatest SNP intellectual of his time. The lesson of these men is to keep our eyes firmly fixed on the best future for our communities, to value the enrichment of the mind from all quarters, to be ready to laugh especially at ourselves. If you want to understand why the Labour party is dear to the hearts of so many people who are not in it, begin by thinking of Michael Foot and John Smith.

But, there are other Labour leaders, some of them still alive and officially (although not certainly) voting NO, yet whom we must salute and whose kinship we must claim. These are the founding fathers of the Scottish Parliament, those whose work began it, and whose stewardship sent it on its way. It is our Parliament and from it constitutionally arose our Referendum once the Scottish people had elected enough MSPs pledged to seeking independence. But that Parliament suffered in its earliest days from unexpected blows: its costs were concealed from the MSPs and its cause was betrayed in a foolish reversal of policy from support to hostility of the then national newspaper *The Scotsman*. Donald Dewar, Henry McLeish and Jack McConnell successively played major parts on all kinds of ways to get the ship of state launched on its maiden voyage, and every one of them deserves the gratitude and respect of their country. Politics are abrasive, journalists are iconoclastic and credit is seldom given save in the praise dished out by sycophants. Any worthwhile history must honour these men.

The cause of Independence is inspired by what was done by our first three First Ministers, but also by what they could not do. From the first it was clear that leadership of a Scottish Parliament would be self-destructive if the leader's eye was fixed on promotion to Westminster, if in fact a seat in the House of Commons was deemed more desirable than one in Holyrood. All of these three wanted to lead Scotland, and to do so from Scotland. Others have sought to make Holyrood a stepping-stone to Westminster, and they have suffered accordingly. They may be prominent when they reach Westminster but their right to speak for Scotland is diminished once they cease to speak in Scotland, or, worse, to resurrect themselves on Westminster off-days in Scottish space with an air of a West End musical slumming in the provinces. However Unionists they may be, Holyrood MSPs have to show they love Holyrood more than Westminster, and that if Westminster wishes (which usually means Whitehall wishes) come first, it is because of the merit in that particular wish, not in the belief that Westminster comes first. It will usually be Westminster MPs from Scottish constituencies (we need not bother with those whom Scots voters sent into legislative exile in England) who are most vehement in public and private that Scotland must always come second. So it was natural that Labour First Ministers found themselves in constant friction with Westminster and Whitehall comrades telling them to knuckle under. Naturally there was the continuation of Westminster/Whitehall historic manipulation of the Scottish parties, with A in London favouring Z as his favourite Scottish voice, B preferring Y, although such favouritism might be circumspect. In pre-Holyrood days even Margaret Thatcher had to show some civility to Malcolm Rifkind, however obviously preferring his mental and moral inferior Michael Forsyth.

And thus it is that the last Labour First Minister, Jack McConnell, while officially advocating NO, knows more reasons to vote YES than perhaps any other member of his party. He is loyal to his party, and he does not reject the merits of the system under which he rose. But he is also loyal to his Parliament, and clearly resented its subordination from time to time on the whim of Whitehall, and had done so before his leadership.

The catastrophic death of Dewar, the unjust forced resignation of McLeish, pushed McConnell into office, as Parliament leader. His patience, his strength, his social conscience played their part in enabling him to gain respect and dignity for the Scottish premiership. But it's not just that he knows the independent judgements by Scots are likely to be sounder on Scottish questions than those of non-Scots made far away. He himself has priorities well outside the limits of a devolved parliamentary leadership. He has, for instance, a passionate hatred of racism under which supposedly independent African countries in particular suffer so badly, however wrapped up in international moneyspeak it may be. He knows that from any standpoint (apart from loony racists') Scotland needs more immigrants as an economic fact as well as a national idea. He is all too aware that on such a matter the Unionist parties in England will twist in the wind of electorally strong prejudice regardless of Labour traditions of humanity and Scottish necessities of economics. If in the end he votes NO, it will probably be No, BUT...

Two years ago, on 14 July 2012, Jack McConnell delivered one of the finest speeches of his life, at the funeral of Dr Bob McLean, his best man. He also wrote McLean's obituary in the *Scotsman* calling him:

> a big man, in every sense of the word. He had a big heart, a massive presence, a wonderful sense of humour, a huge intellect, and a burning passion for Scottish Home Rule. He was one of the most significant extra-parliamentary figures of late twentieth-century Scotland, and his skills placed him at the centre of the campaign to secure a Scottish Parliament. He was the beating heart of the devolution movement, inside and outside the Scottish Labour Party. He was patriotic, a socialist, a true friend...he inspired us, educated us and organised us into the generation that turned his dream into reality...Scotland will always be a better place for the time he spend with us here.

Owen had been Bob McLean's supervisor at Edinburgh for his Ph.D, on the impact of Michael Collins's memory on the ten years of Irish history after his death in 1922, Jack McConnell quoting him on Bob's being a supervisor's dream, a student with the mind of a pioneer. Bob cut his way through a jungle of concealments, reservations, proscriptions, denials of access to documents, reluctant interviewees, data supposedly sealed until

God knows when and survivors who would speak to nobody. His greatness of heart enveloped others, so that what had seemed impossible suddenly seemed the obvious thing to do. He had been election agent for successive Midlothian Labour MPs and an MSP. And he was the living and large embodiment of the neglected truth that nuts and bolts party workers may be passionately interested in political ideas, all the more because they know the detail of where and how they are fighting. He knew, professionally the power of recent history on the minds of survivors.

None of us know how Bob McLean would have voted had we been lucky enough to keep him until September 18th 2014. He had been an SNP supporter in his teens before they met, as had McConnell, both of them responsive to the nationalist Spring in the mid-1970s in which they and many of like mind went over to the Labour party during the SNP civil wars which ended in the expulsion of Stephen Maxwell, Alex Salmond, Kenny MacAskill and others (later readmitted on legal technicalities). McConnell's pre-eminence for the word 'patriot' to describe Bob McLean ways much of both of them: they would have denied the SNP the right to question the patriotism of political opponents, but once, like many others of that generation, had, however briefly accepted the idea of Scottish independence. Jack McConnell organised a lecture in Bob's memory and invited Trevor Phillips to give it. Phillips discussed pros and cons of Scottish independence, making it very clear that since he was not a Scot, and not a voter in the Referendum, he was not taking sides, but he made an exception in one aspect. He told us that if Scotland voted YES a policy of open doors to immigrants was essential, for the social health of a country as for its economic needs. Here, and here alone, he was prepared to say that Scotland gave him greater confidence than he could have in the UK. As for Jack McConnell, we can simply say that he showed himself a good friend, and a patriot.

Whatever the size of the YES vote, it will be have originated in far broader origins than any one, two or three political parties. We will take a final example of a great Scot who did not live as long as the Referendum. The Labour party and Left-wing leaders in general had actually differed greatly on devolution and some, such as Neil Kinnock and Robin Cook had been in the forefront against, in 1979, and for, in 1997. And there were some officially for, and actually against, such as James Callaghan and Tony Blair, while others such as Michael Foot, John Smith, and Gordon Brown, had worked themselves to the bone for it. In the larger Labour movement, the charismatic head of the Scottish miners had been Mick McGahey, a formidable Communist in combat, a genial one in private whether endowing historical research on the miners or exchanging memories with Ted Heath on their days as altar boys (Anglo-Catholic and Roman Catholic). The election of 1997 had been intended by Tony Blair to be a rejection of the Tories without Labour commitment to specific programmes, where possible, but by making it a mandate on devolution, John Major torpedoed that hope and with it, the Tory party in Scotland. Labour in Scotland headed by Donald Dewar had in any case tied itself to the demand for the strongest Parliament as yet on offer, in the Constitutional Convention of 1989 in the Hall of the General Assembly of the Church of Scotland (without whom we might never have had devolution). After his election in 1997 Blair therefore let it be known that while a victory in the Referendum for a Scottish Parliament was desirable (by this stage he had to be officially for it) the majority ought not to be too great. So little meetings were convened with little publicity. Once such happened at the old Royal High School towering over Edinburgh. It was presided over by one non-cabinet Labour MP, and at least one other was there. Everyone was very polite. It was rather like a mothers' meeting in Morningside to discuss a children's party with genteel pronouncements on preferable presents or prizes.

And then there arose from the body of the kirk Michael McGahey at whose appearance the organisers paled in the manner of the Sleeping Beauty's parents when the wicked fairy appears at the christening. Not that Mick made any mention of magic needles, or any other extra-legal forms of persuasion. On the contrary, he was as bland and as enlightened as any eighteenth-century Scottish statesman. Almost flicking a speck of dust from the irreproachable Mechlin lace at his wrists, he beamed on the assembly and remarked with an abstracted air of a man trying to remember a punch-line of an irrelevant joke that the meeting had not been very well publicised and he himself had only heard of it when he was on a bus. It was, he knew, absurd to imagine the organisers would have been trying to keep its existence from him. The organisers, with a rather ghastly set of giggles, attempted to agree that it was absurd. The audience, which evidently knew better, gave vent to the first of many howls of delight and admiration. Mick McGahey then gave us a speech which may well have been the greatest of that Referendum. He told us of the reactionary shambles to which Thatcherism had reduced Scotland, and he told us of the Scotland that could will itself into being, and the greed it must destroy and the good that it must do. He had, after all, seen the cause of nationalism finally achieve reality inside the Communist world. Like many another leader of workers, he had remained in the party while countless others had left, but his continuing after 1990 in the Communist party of Scotland realised his increasing sense of Scottish Miners' interests' divergence from the showy confrontationalism of Arthur Scargill. He had been a leader in the Scottish miners' strike in 1984–85 where they drank tea with the local Police until the London Met arrived with their Alsatians. He had sought Scotland's right to decide whether it would strike. He had subscribed to the Constitutional Convention's demand for a strong Scottish Parliament. And now he told us to believe in it, fight for it, and make a country with it. The crowd loved it, some of us risking necks to hug him when he finished. But he seemed to be looking far beyond the horizons of that Referendum. The cancer, which was devouring him as he spoke killed him eighteen months later.

We are very conscious of the speed of developments, some more unexpected than others. Peter Kilfoyle, of Liverpool, Labour MP for 20 years and junior Minister for Defence under Blair, declared for the YES cause pointing out that its victory in Scotland would be a Godsend to England whose northern and western regions are starved of power and influence while London interests prospered. What he said makes sense and symbolically he makes sense as well. He has an original and independent mind. He is of Irish descent and Catholic belief. He is eleventh of 15 children, worked as a labourer for five years then qualified as a school teacher working for ten, and a passionate opponent of renewing Trident. His predecessor in his Liverpool Walton seat was the old Socialist warhorse Eric Heffer, a grand man for quoting Robert Burns but also a thunderous opponent of Scottish devolution. Kilfoyle shows us that Labour in England,

Labour from Irish roots, Labour of cabinet credentials, Labour in Socialist heartlands can see the democratic victory awaiting England once Scotland has broken through. Scotland outlawing Trident could be very infectious. This magnificently reverses the old Labour cliché about Lanark having more in common with Liverpool than either could have with Moray or Nairn. Liverpool Labour has everything in common with Lanark, above all the democratic Socialist necessity for YES.

Peter Kifoyle of course knew how much Liverpool has in common with Dublin, sometimes called its biggest suburb. Irish independence made no real difference to that. Even the local Liverpool Irish Home Rule MP, T.P. O'Connor, was re-elected for the next eight years. And the Beatles could sound very Irish in Dublin ears.

Much of the debate has been foolishly predicated on the assumption that if Scotland vote YES, the SNP will form subsequent governments. There is no proof of any such thing. Although the SNP supplies the largest single group supporting YES, there are many other YES persons of other parties and of no party. If Scotland votes YES it will be grateful to the SNP for helping that victory, but gratitude for past deeds doesn't necessarily win the next election. The Second Reform Act, which was the first stage in enactment of UK democracy, was won by Disraeli in 1867, but the newly enfranchised voters voted for Gladstone in 1868. Churchill was justly hailed as a national hero in saving the country in World War II, but he and his party were voted from power in the 1945 election that followed it. Labour in independent Scotland has good chances.

CHAPTER ONE

Realising Labour Values

JEANE FREEMAN

SO, WHY NOT? Thinking about why the official position of the Labour Party in Scotland and the UK is to oppose independence is to tap in to the emotional and intellectual struggle that so many Labour members and supporters have had – and are having – in this independence debate.

I grew up supporting the Labour Party. For a time, I was a Labour member and for four privileged years I worked for the party when it was in government at Holyrood. What drew me to Labour politics were the values of social justice, fairness and equality. And it is my continued belief in those values that leads me to support independence now, in 2014. It is not a backward looking support, clinging to the 'old days'. It's not based on centuries' old grudges against ancient wrongs – real and perceived – or a romantic notion of a people 'freed'. It is a pragmatic assessment of how best those values can be realised in my lifetime.

For me, the case for independence is, in a sense, quite simple. Scotland is a nation and for 300 or so years we have been part of a union. For many of those years, many people living in Scotland did well from that union. But in the past decades, that has increasingly not been the case. Successive Westminster governments have failed to use their powers to redistribute wealth, or to systematically deliver equality of opportunity to the citizens of this country. Of course, improvements have been made and some progress secured over that time. But not enough. This is partly because the fundamental political and economic model on which that union is based has remained largely unchallenged and largely unchanged. Those who were rich have become richer, those who were poor have become poorer. In the middle, some have won through to the top but the majority has struggled and continues to struggle to keep their heads just above water. We have not yet challenged the fundamental notion on which all of this is based – that if you just work hard enough, are 'clever' enough and try hard enough, you'll do fine. And if you don't make it, it's because you didn't try hard enough or work long enough or weren't able enough.

Now in 2014, as part of the UK, we are actively encouraged to keep on blaming each other. So unemployment is the 'fault' of those who arrive on our shores and take our jobs and food banks are the 'fault' of those who can't manage their money responsibly. The financial crash and the justification that has been offered for austerity economics are the 'fault' of those of us who borrowed too much, in mortgages or on credit. We are discouraged from talking about zero contract hours, their impact on poor wage rates or the de-regulation of banks and financial services is seldom coherently offered as underlying the employment position or the parlous economic state of the UK. The message is: let's be divided and blame each other. The values of fairness or social justice play no part in this economic model or the political model that promotes it.

And what of equality? After 40-odd years, I've come to the conclusion that it's not enough to argue the rational, logical case. It's not enough to ask, nicely or otherwise. I'm tired of simply accepting the small moves that have been made and then, all too often, taken away again when those in power think it safe to do so. We live in a union that is the fourth most unequal in the western world. A union where the wages gap between men and women is the highest in Europe, and where our pensioners are the poorest and our childcare and transport costs the highest.

Independence brings the opportunity of a written constitution. We don't have that yet. But we could. We could have a constitution that enshrines equality and fairness. A constitution that promotes both our rights and our responsibilities towards each other. And a constitution that sets out the values we will run our country by – and on which we will take our place in the world, without weapons of mass destruction, but with a realistic view of our international role and an ethical foreign policy designed to achieve that. Independence offers us the opportunity to re-think the economic model that has proven itself regressive in every sense. The opportunity to recognise that public investment – in childcare, house building, using our natural resources to build up funds for major infrastructure projects – is precisely that, investment. Not good money thrown after bad, but our money raised from our taxes and the taxes of the businesses who use our talents and energies and abilities to grow. Our public money used to invest in our country and the present and future lives of those who live here – not used to pay off a Westminster government deficit that is rising precisely because the economic model of the union isn't working and those in power are unwilling to change it.

No-one anymore really, seriously argues that Scotland could not be economically and financially independent – and prosperous to boot. The argument now isn't that we couldn't – it's that we shouldn't. But, again, why not? The arguments presented are interesting. The first is, to say the least, a bit ironic. Having castigated the proponents of independence as 'harking back', 'romantic', creating an 'idealised version' of our history, we are now invited to remain in the Union because we have come through so much together. We have, of course, and some of it, such as creating a national health service, defeating fascism in World War II, building a welfare system to protect vulnerable people and those in need, has been hugely positive. But the past is no reason not to take hold of and be in charge of change in our future. Not least when the facts of our daily lives are the dismantling of that welfare system and, south of the Border, the systematic unpicking of our NHS – an NHS that increasingly exists in name only but in reality moves day by day far away from its founding principles.

The second argument against independence, aimed directly at all of us who believe so passionately in fairness and social justice, is the 'stay and fight' argument. Wait for 2015. Work hard for a Labour victory and all will be well. Except it won't. Not with public commitments from the UK Labour shadow cabinet that they will, in government, continue the economic model that has brought so much misery to so many. Not while they insist they will maintain, and indeed increase, the cuts in welfare support that are taking the feet from under thousands of families across Scotland and pushing more children – now one in four – into poverty.

The third is 'let's not waste our energy on all this constitutional stuff, it's a diversion and will all take too long to do'. But this debate is not some dry, boring discussion about dull words and legalities – it's about completing the powers we have in Scotland to make the decisions that affect people who live and work here, and to make those decisions closer to the grain of who we are. And as for time, it took a Labour government only one parliamentary term to create the National Health Service from scratch – and against howling opposition from an establishment that did not want to give up power. Sound familiar? The NHS was the result of a Labour government prepared to be audacious enough to deliver on the values and work in the interests of the people it represented.

Yet, for those of us who have for so long supported Labour, there is another argument to confront: that independence is a 'dirty' word – dirtied by its association with the Scottish National Party. The SNP, the opposition (for some, an opposition even more egregious than the Tories). We have imbibed that sentiment unthinkingly for many years. It plays to our sense of loyalty, to sticking by what we know and what those before us stood for. But let's stop and think this one through.

Political parties are created to give voice to shared beliefs and values. To express those values and beliefs in political action and in the exercise of the power voters lend to politicians. They are not an end in themselves but a means to an end. So when a political party no longer acts to fulfil those values, we owe it no loyalty. We owe loyalty to our values and our beliefs, to ourselves and to each other. Neither Scotland nor the people who live here 'belong' to any political party. And our independence will not 'belong' to any political party either. The decision we will make on the September 18 is a decision about whether the Scotland we want to live in is best served by independence or by staying as a part of the UK. It's a decision we will make not just for ourselves but for our families, our children, our communities and Scotland's future generations.

If there is one thing the decline in voting numbers and the angst over political disengagement tells us, it is this: people going about the business of living – going to work or finding a job, feeding families or looking after children – are not interested in political point-scoring or clever wheezes to show up one side of the argument or the other as foolish or wrong. They are not interested in name-calling or the rapid-fire exchange of statistics. More than disinterested, in fact, they are utterly alienated by it. It is from this that the 'they're all the same', and the 'it's got nothing to do with me' sentiments come. And who in truth can blame them?

And if that applies to most folk it applies doubly to women. Frankly, women haven't the time or the patience for behaviour that we grew out of when we left the playground. For a moment, forget the research, forget the private polling, forget the lengthy political treatises about what wins elections and what doesn't. Just think of your own life. Do you want to surround yourself by the folk who tell you 'you cannae dae that' and 'it'll never work'? If women had listened to these folks in years gone by we'd never have won a smidgen of equality and we'd certainly never have won the right to vote. But we didn't, because, simply, we can't afford to. We've too much to do and too many daily problems to solve to waste time giving up. So the unsurprising news is that scare stories – great, small and at times downright ridiculous – are pretty poor substitutes for genuine, engaging, down-to-earth conversations.

In the past two years, as a result of the discussion and debate in Scotland on independence, we have seen something quite remarkable happen. A genuine grassroots movement is emerging, growing and acting. Young and old, with radical and conservative ideas. People in cities and towns and villages. On our mainland and our islands. People arguing for independence from their own life experiences – as business men and women, artists, writers, musicians, actors, lawyers, environmentalists, academics and taxi drivers. And in all of these groups and more, women's voices are coming through loud and, increasingly, clear. Women's voices encouraged, supported and promoted by the grassroots 'Women for Independence' campaign, a group started over two years ago by a small number of women from across all political parties and none which has grown in numbers and strength beyond anyone's expectation.

These voices ask questions, seek out information, weigh up arguments. But they also paint their own picture of the kind of country we want to live in – in our own colours and our own words. By running street work, engaging with groups, using social media, talking in ones and twos and in hundreds, we are collecting the ideas and hopes of people throughout Scotland. This is far removed from the back biting and petty point scoring most associate with mainstream politics.

A quick look at what folk have come up with so far shows a remarkable degree of agreement. But more than that, it shows that when the question is asked, no-one needs to go away and ponder for weeks before they answer. People in Scotland know the kind of country they want for themselves and their families. They just need to be asked. And then, through grassroots activity, they gain the confidence to put their answers into practice. And the first step in that is a vote for independence. This is the real challenge. To end our practice of voting (or not) every few years and then leaving it to the politicians to get on with it. Independence is not about having more of the same but with tartan round it. It offers all of us the chance to create a country built on those values of fairness, social justice and equality. But it also demands of us that we remain engaged and involved, and it demands of our political system that it changes to really devolve power and to engage in co-operation and action for 'the common weal'. That's a challenge to every political party – Unionist or otherwise.

So what is the answer to the question, 'Why not?' That the Union has always worked for us and always will? It hasn't, it won't and the historical gains we have made in that union are increasingly threatened. Is the answer that it will all be sorted if we only hold fire and vote Labour in the Westminster election in 2015? No, not with the UK Labour commitments already made to keep the failed economic model and the discredited political model of the past decades.

Is the answer to remember that we all hate nationalism and that our loyalty demands a NO vote? Independence is no party's prize. Independence is about asserting our own right to govern ourselves, and no party loyalty is greater than our loyalty to ourselves and our values. Is the answer that it's not 'our place' to do these things, to take decision-making power into our own hands? No, because in each of the past 15 years of devolution, we have shown we can make good decisions for our country and there is no-one better able to make the right decisions for the people of Scotland than those of us who live here.

For me, there is no credible answer to the 'Why not?' question. Independence is about choice – choosing to trust ourselves, choosing to have confidence that we can run our own affairs, choosing to build our country anew. So, again: why not?

CHAPTER TWO

War and Peace

OWEN DUDLEY EDWARDS

The sword sung on the barren heath
The sickle sung in the fruitful field.
The sword he sung a song of death
But could not make the sickle yield.

WILLIAM BLAKE 1757–1827

SCOTLAND MUST CHOOSE between a warfare state and a welfare state.

That is what is at stake between voting YES for Independence or voting NO to it. It is a question of priorities.

Do you want to be part of a country which sees its main reason for existence to nourish its people and the people of the world?

Or do you want to be part of a country which sees its main reason for existence that it can threaten the world with annihilation and that the welfare of its citizens and the world must take second place to manufacturing, storing and selling the means of death?

Trident is the obvious place to see where we separate.

When the politicians who want to keep Scotland in the UK tell us why, the pivot is that the UK has the fourth largest defence establishment in the world. And this, they believe, is the main reason for Scotland to remain in the United Kingdom. The Prime Minister, Mr David Cameron, seems a kindly and good-natured person. Unlike many leading Unionist agitators in the Unionist parties – Tories, Labour, Liberal Democrats, UKIP, BNP, etc., etc., – he isn't really a bully. It is true he had to qualify for his job by outrageous exhibitions of bad temper and foul manners when Leader of the Opposition during 'Prime Minister's Questions' in the Westminster Parliament, and such matters have not noticeably improved since he became Prime Minister. His followers and their opponents spend more decibels making noises which no zoo could tolerate than in making any intelligible sound whatsoever. But he is normally courteous and likeable in manner. If he is jeered at for going to a 'posh' school, Eton, or his parents or both turned out a fairly civilised product, which is more than most other public schoolmen in his cabinet can claim. Most of us might not have much in common with him, but he gives a sense of good nature, and if his primary interest in us is to get our votes, he really makes you feel that he would like you to mean more to him than he is able to imagine.

The world in which Mr Cameron lives may be less useful to his electoral fortunes than he imagines, but he certainly doesn't need its expertise to tell him under no circumstances to debate in public with Mr Salmond. That lethal slingshot, the Salmond sense of humour, is quite beyond Mr Cameron's powers. He knew he had to be circumspect in dealing with, say, the interrogation methods of Jeremy Paxman. Mr Salmond simply withered Mr Paxman with sweetness and light ('Why don't you let me finish my sentence, Jeremy, and then you can patronise it?'), Mr Cameron may not be the world's greatest debater, but he knows how to finish as a good third, that is if he can't win on his own he can squeeze a coalition from it.

But that terrible laughter Mr Salmond would prompt gives Mr Cameron no chance. For one thing, he forgot how to laugh like that when he forgot what it had meant to his remote ancestors to be Scots. He knows about Scots regiments, Scots guards, and possibly even Scots claymores. But his vision of Scotland stops short at imagining the weapons of peace. It is all the sadder because the Camerons really are worth talking about — that is to say, the older ones were. But their descendant shows no sign of being able to talk about them. If he hugs the UK it is partly because it is the only way he can think about the place his ancestors came from. He talks of the UK having four nations, and so do his messenger-boys. He and his unworthy disciples explain that these four nations are England, Scotland, Wales and Northern Ireland oblivious of the fact that the inhabitants of Northern Ireland sustained thirty years of murderous warfare to deny that they were one nation. The error is simple enough: the UK was formed piecemeal by Wales, England, Scotland and Ireland, and in theory that left the basis for a foursome. But since the Unionist think-tanks want to sell the UK as a Union between Scotland and England, ignoring as much of its real history as possible, Northern Ireland has to be declared a nation when mentioned at all. Similarly it was ignored for the Olympic Games so that the Unionists could sell their product as 'Team GB'.

If they had the sense to declare 'Team UK' they might have a better chance of Northern Ireland beginning to think of itself as a nation. But if its nationality consists only in being available for chorus work occasionally breaking aeons of endless oblivion, what is the point of it? Here the agreeable Mr Cameron isn't the best witness for Scotland's identity inside the UK. If Scotland really and truly means so little to him apart from kilts where the other UKanians wear breeks, is this the future that awaits it in the UK? Are we to have an endless future of amnesiac Scots who know it is very important that they are Scots although why, nobody will be able to remember except that whatever we were or weren't wearing, we killed a lot of people in the process? This is less necessary today since we have Trident to do it for us.

And, if we declare our independence, we cannot have Trident at all. This debate has involved a lot of misinformation, some of it disinformation. The YES people have told us Independence means goodbye to Trident, some NO people have speculated that in such an event maybe for Scotland to procrastinate in losing Trident could be a means of persuading the UK to facilitate what it has agreed to do in any case. But the matter is settled beyond all negotiation. Scotland once independent becomes a new country bound by international law.

And under international law no country which does not at present possess weapons of mass destruction may acquire or possess such weapons. That independent Scotland will have been a portion of the UK, doesn't mean that this new Scotland can have a bit of Trident any more than it means it can have all of Trident. The political parties now leading the YES campaign abominate Trident being wise and honest people. But even they were as silly and dishonest as governments who have such weapons, Scotland cannot have Trident. It is possible that some Unionists may take their silliness so far as to say, 'oh but when we said no country lacking weapons of mass destruction may have them, we only meant that to justify our insisting Iraq could not have them, or Iran could not have them, or North Korea could not have them, you can't think we meant to apply the law to ourselves, whether all of ourselves or bits of ourselves?'. Their case breaks down before their lips have finished the sentences, leaving them open to sentences of a rather different kind. Someone should tell the UK Defence Secretary, for instance, that if he continues to insist Scotland will have to keep Trident on its soil or in its waters at the UK's command irrespective of its independence, then he is surely in danger of engaging in conspiracy to defeat the ends of justice, and that he may have to answer not to Scotland, but Scotland Yard. That should make him think a little: Scotland Yard is not at its friendliest towards his party these days.

This illegality under new ownership is a fact, with a battery of UN resolutions behind it, treaties, understandings, and the lot. And here let's look at some of the misinformation/ disinformation used on the issue by Unionists active or passive. Unionists demand to know where the UK government should put Trident when it is expelled from Scottish soil and Scottish waters. We ought to refrain from answering that question with coarse personal suggestions as to its disposal, and in fact it is none of our business. We were not consulted when nuclear weapons were imposed by the UK government on Scottish soil and Scottish seas, and we are unlikely to be consulted now. If it was none of our business when it really was our business, it is certainly none of our business when it is no longer our business. The analogy is presumably that of a householder who let some part of his grounds to a neighbour on a system of joint occupancy, decisions as to furnishing of the joint occupancy being made by the neighbour without consultation. (Put like that, it seems to make the original owner a bit of a fat-head, but we all make mistakes). Anyhow, the lease has been terminated, the jointly occupied property reverts to the original owner. Meanwhile the grounds jointly occupied involved the placing of a grotesque pagan idol of gross indecency and capable of emitting substances dangerous to human life, and now the original owners say it is not their property and is not to remain on their property. There is no point in which the former tenant has the right to maintain the noxious horror on his former premises for any length of time. Presumably the UK will have to relocate Trident in another part of the UK. But no other part of the UK may want it, and while the government may seek to force Cornwall or Wales to house it, they may encounter more sophisticated local resistance.

Mind you, Scottish denial of Whitehall's right to turn the place into a haven or a dump for nuclear weapons had long term effects. It was the Labour party whose members took the lead in anti-nuclear demonstrations in the 1960s and after, and Scotland should be proud of them! But many future Scottish Nationalists and some already in the SNP also were CND activists from the first, and the first SNP MP elected at a general election was Donald Stewart, the Lord Provost of Stornoway, who captured the parliamentary seat in 1970 when his people rose to protest the way Whitehall wantonly turned their vulnerable civilisation into a target and a nuclear arsenal which threatens with destruction of what it purports to preserve. Compton Mackenzie's novel *Rockets Galore* records the anger and determination of that revolt.

But we can all take comfort in the thought that Scotland will be saving itself by its exertions and (to adopt a phrase of the Younger Pitt) may save the rest of the UK by its example. Much Unionist rhetoric consists of an endless proliferation of the same clichés, many of which were already thoroughly shop-worn after the 1979 Referendum, when the Tories promised a stronger Scottish Parliament for those who voted No and the Labour Party dissidents amended the Referendum resolution so that when Scotland had voted for its Parliament, it was deemed not to have done so.

In those years the Labour dissidents were endlessly intoning that they felt a unity between workers in Glasgow and Gateshead, between Dundee and Darlington. It has been regurgitated endlessly in 2014 with all the intellectual profundity of senile ventriloquists' dummies. The answer is that the Scots seek independence affirming their comradeship to workers in Delhi as well as Dundee and Darlington, and Gdansk as well as Glasgow and Gateshead. And Scottish Independence could result in a far greater liberation than mutual cross-Border support as alibis for inaction. For the end of Trident means the end of prioritising WMD at the expense of the National Health, and of the Welfare benefits for the impoverished and disadvantaged, and of the necessary investment in education without imprisoning our students for life under mountains of debt, and of the care and pensions to which the aged who have served us so long are entitled, and of the needful measures to play our part as well as we can in saving our planet. We will be delighted if our action frees the UK from its own nuclear self-destruction but the way to do it is by saving ourselves rather than stewing in a hopeless inertia at the behest of politicians who have done quite well for themselves out of the Union and want to go on doing it.

One of the more ludicrous arenas employed by the Unionists is the House of Lords in which, by an interesting coincidence, none of the Scottish political parties campaigning for YES will permit themselves to sit. This therefore means that Unionists can luxuriate in Upper Chamber debate, during which it becomes increasingly difficult to distinguish between them and the plush beneath their behinds. Their ladyships and lordships receive £150 per day of attendance in their House if they are doing nothing, £300 if while present they engage in Parliamentary business. Presumably participation in a debate qualifies you for your daily £300, as would voting in a debate, and possibly emission of rather more aristocratic or at least refined noises to the same effect as those employed by the cruder Commons. Certainly the £300 would have been due by the UK taxpayer when their ladyships and their lordships decided to have a 'debate' on Scottish independence. None of them seems to have pointed out that in the event of Scottish independence the Scottish taxpayer will not pay out one penny to enable a set of old parties in fancy dress to continue to flourish their profundities with not a belch of opposition.

The gallantry of these proceedings are relative: their lordships and ladyships tell one another how valuable their contributions had been, but however akin to the courage and spirit of the 300 at Thermopylae, nobody would be likely to mention the 300 even dearer to them (and certainly, dearer to the rest of us). There is also a simple matter of self-gratification. Their lordships and ladyships savour the value of telling themselves how fortunate the UK is to have had their services, what an honour it has been for the UK to reward them, and what a tragedy for the UK it would have been had they not played so noble a part in public life. They have various committee hearings at which they can tell one another how bestial the thought of the Lordless Scottish Independence, but on 30 January 2014 they solemnly 'took note of the implications for the United Kingdom of the forthcoming Scottish independence referendum'.

The 'debate' was opened, and the necessity of taking note moved, by Lord Lang of Monklands, formerly a star of Fringe comedy for the Cambridge Footlights, less formerly Secretary of State for Scotland and so on up until ultimately dispensed with by his electors in 1997 when like most of his fellow debaters he had been exhorting the Scottish electorate to realise that their own devolved Parliament would be bad for them. The voters in fact decided he had served his Thatcher better than his country, and most of the ermined ghosts around him have bitten the same dust. The debate was duly printed in *Hansard*, with the usual privilege by which those Lords who preferred not to have said what they had said, could delete it or amend it at will. (No doubt the proof-correction or record-falsification always qualifies parliamentary business.) In any event it had (seemed good to Lord Lang in opening the debate to declare that if Scotland voted for independence it would dishonour the dead UK soldiers who had been killed in the first World War. Whether it dishonoured the war dead more by this form of posthumous exploitation there were none to enquire, but an STV interviewer after the debate politely commented to her interviewee, Lord Forsyth, of Drumlean, Lord Lang's successor as Secretary of State for Scotland, in his case that job being curtailed by his electoral defeat in 1997.

They were indeed a true storehouse of wisdom and value since, as a result of them, no Scottish Tory has ever been elected to the House of Commons since 1997 save a solitary MP in each subsequent Parliament: but in 1997 itself the future Lords Lang, Forsyth, etc. were blotted out, not to say exorcised. But Lord Forsyth whose reaction to earlier defeats when in power had been to declare that Scotland needed more Thatcherism, not less, and prescribe for the patient accordingly, now in 2014 showed that his retirement had diminished none of his contempt for democracy. He informed his STV host that Lord Lang had made no such remark. She assured him that she had heard and seen him say it in the televised debate, Lord Forsyth repeated that Lord Lang had made no such remark. And when *Hansard* was published, no such remark was there. The whole episode was a rather chilling reminder of how thoroughly we have adopted the public obliteration of fact in Orwell's *1984*.

But the logic of the argument Lord Lang so successfully unsaid merits some attention also. The cynicism of the whole exercise, the debate which did not debate, the thing said which subsequently had not been said, the deference paid to hallowed altruism amounting to exultation in their own plunder – one felt sorry for Mr Cameron and Mr Alistair Darling, who bear the heat of the day. They at least are enemies inviting some respect.

But the grossness and subsequent cowardice of the Lang-Forsyth dishonour of the World War 1 dead cannot by contrast absolve Prime Minister Cameron, however superior morally he is to either peer. His genuine anxiety to express his love for the UK is forever dragged back to the slaughterhouse; his insistence on the glorious history bled in the ranks of death he finds its supreme justification. What Lord Lang permitted himself to have said after emasculation by Lord Forsyth, was in harmony with Mr Cameron's thought if not with his taste. The sanitised Lang concluded that what he had said was:

> For generations, Scots and English have lived alongside each other, sharing a British heritage. They fought shoulder to shoulder in the battles of the past three centuries and still serve together today; we all take pride in that. Together, they built and administered the empire before turning it into the Commonwealth, with Scots very much to the fore. Both countries are woven into the fabric of the UK. Must they now, both Scotland and England, disavow that shared history? Would that not dishonour the sacrifices, made in common cause, of those who died for the United Kingdom, a nation now to be cut in two if the present generation of Scottish nationalists have their way? I earnestly hope not.

If Lord Lang 'earnestly' saw his fellow-peers as his primary audience, his estimate of their collective intelligence must be pretty low. On his logic the Scots have been consistently dishonouring the Scottish dead, of God knows how many battles of the Scots against English, by being in the Union at all. From *Y Gododdin* in 600 AD to Dunbar in 1650 he would have the brave-hearts resurrecting themselves in indignation, to say nothing of Butcher Cumberland's meat from 1746. It is a revolting example of Unionist political contempt for their supporters. Of course the UK did much good, and it also did some harm, and the same may be said for any country or coalition of countries.

The notion that legislation today dishonours a remote yesterday is nonsense, although it certainly dishonours the dead to recruit them as prostitutes in our service. All people in these islands, whatever their constitutional status then and now, should be very proud of the British and Northern Irish people who maintained morale and human solidarity while death was raining down on their heads in World War II. All of us should be truly grateful to the Attlee government of 1945–51 probably the best one in these islands in the entire century, and in order to prevent its dishonour by a modern generation pulling its heroic health system to pieces in the interest of their warfare state, the best thing is for Scotland to become a state with true welfare priorities.

The defence of the Union is in ungrateful hands. We who want Scotland independent want that partly because it's the surest way to hold on to some of the best things the UK did, and from that point of view those who call for independence love the UK best. What most Unionists tributes to the UK do, apart from silly schoolboy stuff about being the strongest and the nicest and the best, is to talk of an imaginary history which never could exist. It is simply insulting to the people of these islands to call their history the best, since it's clear that those who claim this really know nothing about these islands' history, and since they don't trouble to learn what it really is, apparently don't give a damn about it. To say that the UK is the best union there ever was is to say that the earth is flat, the moon is made of green cheese, and, as the first gravedigger says in *Hamlet*, the English are all mad. All these things are absurd, but it's quite easy to argue they are true, especially doing so for £300 a day in the House of Lords with nobody to contradict you. We can certainly recognise that the UK did much good, if sometimes unfeeling and heartless good, in the name of progress.

You get the same ludicrous exaggeration and the same contempt for listeners, when the Unionists are telling us what will happen to the UK if Scotland votes YES. One standard prediction, sometimes prophesied by otherwise sane and sensible people, is that if Scotland becomes independent the UK will lose its seat on the Security Council of the United Nations, or that it will lose it if it loses Trident. This is gibbering insanity. The UN is an organisation founded for peace, not for the maintenance of arsenals of weapons of mass destruction. The loss of territory has no effect on the UK's seat on the Security Council, which was determined by membership of the wartime alliance, formally known as the United Nations, from 1941 to 1945. When another of the victors in that alliance, the USSR, lost its formal title and enormous tracts of its territory and population from 1990, not the slightest question existed of its losing its place on the Security Council. Lord Lang, only a few paragraphs into his speech to the Lords, told their listening lordships and ladyships:

> The once-united kingdom would shrink, not just physically but in the eyes of the world. Others would see it as diminished: diminished in size, diminished in population, diminished in strength and diminished in authority. The mother of parliaments would be viewed as crumbling and Britain's international prestige and influence would crumble with it. Our standing in the Commonwealth would change, our standing in Europe, in NATO, the UN, the World Bank and the World Trade Organisation – one could go on.

No doubt one could. One might begin by fearing the crumbling of the international reputation of the House of Lords if this is the way its members justify their £300 *per diem*. All of this diminution of territory happened over Ireland between 1922 and 1949, and what did the world say? The world found it a great relief that the UK had at last come to some sort of solution over its own disputed territory at its own heartland. The world was wrong, because the settlement was badly made in important ways, so much so that the century ended with thirty years' war in Northern Ireland. As is happened, the international stature of the UK has never been higher than in 1940. Winston Churchill –who really did know what history was – called it our finest hour. If we add in the Labour legislation of the same decade, in and out of his Government, it certainly was. And the logic of the Thatcher Unionists would say that the people then were cold and forced to ration food and bombed out of their house and home, and much too concerned with other parts of the world, so what good was it? That generation will be remembered and thanked by those who cherish its ideals - the advocates of Scotland's independence rather than the latter-day Thatcherites. The mother of Parliaments would increase its standing when it was realized that the Scottish half of the island of Britain was no longer governed at the command of the Tories for not more than one of whom had they voted. And if Lord Lang wanted to know what did diminish the status of the mother of parliaments, let him look at his fellow Thatcherite future minister who in 1976 seized the mace of the Speaker of the House of Commons in order to murder the then prime minister. (No doubt the man was drunk at the time but it wasn't nice.) If he wants to save the mother of Parliaments he can begin by telling its Unionist personnel to stop behaving like ill-trained animals. As for the status of the UK in Europe, it is unlikely to sink as low as it did under Prime Minister Thatcher whose incessant boorishness and offensiveness to all the heads of government in other European powers left the UK known as the sick man of Europe.

But in any case the Prime Minister would be well advised to keep his connections with almost all participants in the Lords debate as purely ceremonial. He seems too kindly a soul to tell his seniors that it was they who landed him in the present mess, but he knows it, and so do they. The Tory Lordships who served Thatcher and Thatcherism have only to recall the dismal electoral figures (dismal for them, not for humanity) to read their political obituaries. Their contemporary Labour grandees are by definition oxymorons: how can Socialists allow themselves to be made lords and ladies? Of those who followed their masters in the Lords' 'debate', Lady Liddell by her abrasiveness, brutality and negative demeanour was a proto-Thatcher while Lord Robertson embodied the Scottish cringe. Perhaps our only evidence suggesting Tony Blair liked practical joking was his nomination of Robertson as Secretary-General of NATO. There were a few speakers whose work getting the Scottish Parliament started had been invaluable, notably Lord Steel for the Liberal Democrats, Lord McConnell for Labour and Lady Goldie for the Tories. Yet their situation was absurd. In the terms of the debate, all participants were numbered on Lord Lang's side, yet these three had worked hard to ensure the infant Scottish Parliament's survival, while the majority of those Lords now denouncing Independence had spent their last Scottish political moments cursing all who sought its birth. As Thatcherites they could not even know what personal independence was, or if they did, had abjured it at the icy commands of their secular queen. So there really was a massive ground for debate in that daft drag drama, positive against negative, constructive against destructive, compassionate against coercive, but not the charade that was performed.

The 'debate' followed the fashion in foretelling the future, and as to that the only certainty about independent Scotland is that it cannot possess Trident. Everything else is no more than speculative. Above all, politicians who foretell the future don't improve their status as truth-tellers. Economists who forecast results of independence might merit more attention if they had forecast the world depression that burst on us early in the 21st century. They were of less use than Biblical scholars who could have pointed out to us that Joseph in Egypt forecast seven lean years following seven fat ones (genesis xii). Indeed some Biblical scholars did.

But as we contemplate a Scotland whose defence is based on the country's needs, instead of lobbyists' attractions and imperial senility to remember whether it is fighting the First or Second Afghan War, we should take a look at a Trident mystery. Who wants it? And why? The NO-men will talk endless economic fairy tales to show that unless we vote NO the Wicked Witch will have us for lunch (and bitch about the cooking). But when we make the obvious point that a Scotland without Trident can afford what the UK is not allowed to spend, a clammy silence descends. In a recent debate Mr Alistair Darling, parroting the usual dismal prophesies, was confronted by the promise of Scottish solvency without Trident and argument died on his lips.

He said that Trident was a very controversial issue that many people felt strongly for it, and many others against it. And he dropped the matter right there. The truth seems to be that nobody wants it, apart from those who directly make money from it, and there have been NO-men who denounce the immorality of getting rid of Trident in view of the jobs it makes.

A country which proclaims that it will devastate vast territories and populations if someone attacks it, is a country proclaiming itself the enemy of humanity. Nobody has the right to use weapons of mass destruction, no country has the right to permit it. The reply that it will never be used because it is there, is morally and mentally contemptible. Many military people say the thing is an utter waste of money, thus weakening sensible priorities. Trident does not and could not aid in a country's defence: it is indefensible, physically or ethically. Yet all the Unionist parties have made it the great and wonderful Oz of their theology, the Baal whom all must bow down and adore. We seem to have become conscripted in some foul rite of potential mass-sacrifice, about which everyone is afraid to talk in ordinary language. The most obvious language to make Unionists understand is 'We cannot afford it'.

Abraham Lincoln wrote – about a year before he was murdered – 'I claim not to have controlled events, but confess: plainly that events have controlled me'. Perhaps the greatest man ever to have become head of state and head of government by the democratic process, he was wise in his humility, and probably had more to do with controlling events than most of us do, but it is sensible to realise that events almost always control us. So we should see what lessons we have to learn since the election closest in time to our Referendum, the election where Scotland like the rest of the European Union voted for its next Members of the European Parliament. The rest of the UK voted for its MEPs in the same Parliament. And the big story of the UK results was that UKIP beat all the other parties, topping the poll in England. In Scotland UKIP crawled into the last available seat, after the SNP 2, the Labour 2, and the Tory 1. The Scottish UKIP vote was slightly over a third of the SNP vote. So Scotland's voters proved themselves radically different from other British voters, particularly those in England.

This in fact continues a UK trend very clear since Thatcher's first UK election in 1979. Scotland voted against Thatcher, by bigger and bigger majorities until the election of 1997 when the now Thatcherised Tories lost every Scottish seat. Now, Thatcherism meant many things repulsive to Scotland. Gordon Brown put his finger on one in the title of his 1989 book *Where there is Greed – Margaret Thatcher and the Betrayal of Britain's Future*. Thatcher appealed to competitive values, essentially telling us we should be trying to do each other down, grabbing each other's throats and handbags, where the Scottish tradition is one of community, of working together for the betterment of society. And Thatcher, of course, announced there was no such thing as society, a silly remark but a very revealing one.

But statistics and votes don't easily translate themselves into philosophical effects however much they really stem from them. And it's worth noting that the 1983 UK Parliamentary election result was anything but certain for Thatcher until she want to war against Argentina, a very vulnerable enemy fool enough to try to seize the Falkland Islands apparently because the ruling junto was led to believe the UK was withdrawing its significant military presence. Thatcher's authorised biography by Charles Moore makes it clear that in the months before she saved herself by saving the Falklands (apart from the soldiers and civilians who lost their lives in the conflict), Thatcher was very vulnerable. Because of her even more than in spite of her, the Tory party was as male chauvinist as any, probably more than most, and while it had weathered her unexpected victory over Ted Heath for the party leadership, if she lost the Election of 1983 the writing would have appeared on the wall for her as it had after the defeat of 1974 for Heath. Her Falklands victory confirmed her in seven more years of leadership life. It was extremely convenient. And what made it crucial was Thatcher's mobilisation of the martial spirit in the English people. She was a ludicrous anachronism in many respects, notably her rhetoric. She prated about Victorian values, knowing little history and valuing it less, but her antennae were good, and she realised that appealing to snob class values meant she should sound like the upper class to which she yearned to belong. The Victorian values most easily transmitted across space and time were the noisy rhetoric of Kipling's cruder poems and the sweaty patriotism pumped out at Music Halls. She served the values up, defrosted and rewarmed, and the Falklands had just enough reality to enable her to do it. She tapped the militaristic keg, and in England at least its intoxicating contents warmed ageing blood. Above all it drove home the argument that to be important, England must flaunt her military and naval spirit. It made the most of World War II cults, and carefully forgot about the truth which was that the chief British and Northern Irish heroes of World War II were the civilian population whose chief anxiety was to save lives, and that the Russians made the greatest sacrifice, and that the Americans were the decisive power in gaining victory. Thatcherism saw synthetic militarism as the surest means of political survival. It saw her through the remainder of her elections, and her successors John Major and Tony Blair found wars in which faithfully to follow her example. But Tory votes diminished and ultimately disappeared in 20th Century Scotland.

There was a xenophobic spirit about UK militarism. In theory it should have cherished the memory of the UK coming to the aid of France and Belgium for love of France and Belgium (frequently visible in surviving soldier letters and diaries). It should have taken high pride in the devotion of so many troops white and non-white from the Empire, it should have relished the fraternal spirit by which the UK was heartened in knowing the Russians were maintaining resistance in Europe, it should have been refreshed by individual stories of the heroism of oppressed peoples under Nazi tyranny, it should have gloried in the American saviours. In practice some imagery seemed to stifle the atmosphere leaving only a vague conviction that the UK had been continually threatened by a Europe united under Napoleon, under the Kaiser Wilhelm II, under Hitler, under Jacques Delors... UK media chauvinised its print repulsively and repetitively as newspaper moguls turned their pressmen into lackeys and their obsessions into creeds and politicians scratched and scrabbled against one another to prove themselves the greatest boy scout of all. The warfare state may be antihuman, but it knows the crudest ways in which to clinch its hold on human emotions. The dotty anti-European crusades needed to climax and to retreat since it frayed if kept at full blast, but the machinery was kept well-oiled by inflammation against immigrants, and even against asylum-seekers, becoming more and more conspiracy – screaming about the wicked outsiders who were coming to steal jobs, prestige, country, welfare, and health. A gospel of hatred may be hard to sustain, but if it is fuelled by continuous worship of the delights of patriotic bloodshed it can regularly renew itself. UKIP victories are the logical result.

But the Euroelection of 2014 told a different Scottish story. It would be nice to live in our own tartan cloud-cuckoo land by denying UKIP could happen here, and up to now we assured ourselves it couldn't. But Scots people are swamped in the same toxic British chauvinism. They show themselves largely immune to it, as they did to Thatcher, the great Earthmother of UKIP, but political health cannot hope to be kept free from epidemics. Scotland rejects the xenophobia and the wars, just as it rejects Trident, and culture that wants to abolish Trident is healthier than one that keeps Trident as its public icon and crown of national glory. But cases do break out, and the virulence of xenophobic infection brings forth its political rashes, and its eczema. In the present aftermath of the Euroelections, Scotland and England have contrasting patterns of official self-interest. Scotland needs immigrants, so the UKIP panic buttons will be fairly easily jammed for want of genuine fuel or electricity. UKIP insist they sell nectar, but their produce is as gut-corrosive as bathtub gin. They may know it too. Nigel Farage may seem as absurd as any demagogue before he gains power. He may seem to renew his strength by political pratfalls. It was all very funny when he was thrown out of an Edinburgh pub for trying to hold an unauthorised press-conference on it, and then had to be given asylum in it as an angry crowd gathered led by an anti-racist Englishman whom Farage then denounced as a Scottish nationalist racist. He enjoys playing the pub bore, waving his pint around like Harold Wilson or Tony Benn with their pipes or Thatcher with her hand bag, and if he sounds a little mad, and more than a little inaccurate, the British are tolerant, as the Prime Minister insists, and they are markedly used to putting up with the obsessions of pub bores.

But on election night there was a moment when we saw the real Nigel Farage. Some question came up about European Parliament procedures and requirements, and suddenly he was a crisp, clear, shrewd, practical authority on his subject. Insofar as he was human, it was not the easy-going loose-lip demagogue giggling that he had said something true but improper. It was an extremely skilled social scientist with mastery of his theory and practice. In a creepy way, he seemed almost to love the institution he gets elected to abolish. In his fashion he is more formidable than the David Camerons and Philip Hammonds, the Ed Ballses and George Osbornes, the Johann Lamonts and Alistair Carmichaels, who so often donate endless amounts of ammunition to the YES camp: Nigel Farage makes Folly his servant where so many other Unionists make it their master. He may not have a sense of humour, but he has a dangerous sense of fun. But in Scotland he faces a society which loves its immigrants, and enjoys its cosmopolitanism (the Edinburgh Festival for one has seen to that), and has learned enough to know that the necessities and privileges of life mean working together against Trident and against the warfare state. Let us keep it so.

Ironically, Nigel Farage, however absurdist in fact, is ominous in theory. His demagogic prowess may be genially clownish, but so, we should remember, was that of US Senator Joe McCarthy, and he has McCarthy's skill in manoeuvring from pratfall to take the offensive in every sense of the term. He showed as much in Edinburgh, where he managed to turn a protest against the racism clinging to UKIP's reputation into insistence that he was the victim of racism hurling his alleged persecution into screeches of denunciation apparently against the Scottish Government, the Scottish People, and anyone who wasn't going to vote UKIP. It is unlikely to get him far in Scotland, although it may have marginally aided the election by a whisker of his personal choice for Scotland the most improbable candidate in the entire UK election for the EU. But the sequel to that election in England was alarming. All three of the major Unionist parties began to talk of the need to reconsider questions of immigration, even to the point of expressions of contrition, however unlikely a confessor Mr Farage may seem. The penance he gives them will contain more scourges than prayers.

This becomes even more sinister when we contemplate the next possible Referendum following that on Scottish Independence. All the major Unionist parties (however minor the next UK election may leave some of them) now produce either barefaced promises or coy hints that if elected they will demand a Referendum on UK membership of the European Community. The Referendum in question shows every probability of being stampeded into a rejection of Europe by the UK electorate. If Scotland is still in the UK it would almost certainly vote strongly in favour of remaining in the EU only to find itself swamped by the mass slaughter of the UK's European identity. Mr Cameron had prevailed with God knows what bribes to articulate various prominent persons in condemnation of Scottish independence. What sacrifices he had to make to get some of these condemnations we do not know, although his success in drawing curses on Caledonia from the People's Republic of China do not suggest that he will be a serious advocate for civil rights in China in the foreseeable future. Equally his success in the creation of European Scotophobes will have deprived his hand of what few EU trump cards are left to it, so that he will have little chance of stemming the Europhobic tide in England which his short-term tactics have consistently fed. He has orchestrated a campaign to make Scottish voters believe Scottish independence would drive them out of the EU. If he should be successful, the next logical stage will be to drive the entire UK out of it. Scottish Europhiles had better realise their hope of remaining in the EU depends on voting YES on 18 September 2014. If Scotland votes No its probable effect will be a No to Scotland's European future. We will be left in the cold clammy dark with UKIP, its Unionist Europhobe disciples, and, of course, Trident. Xenophobia's logical bed chamber is the Warfare State.

CHAPTER THREE

Britain, Global Development and Scotland

DUNCAN MaCLAREN

I HAVE BEEN ASKED to write about a subject that, politically, has minority status in most countries of the world, including, shamefully, the UK. Yet, along with climate change, it is the greatest moral challenge of our time. The issue is global poverty which, as Ruth Lister writes, 'disfigures and constrains the lives of millions of men, women and children and its persistence diminishes those among the non-poor who acquiesce or help sustain it'.[1] In other words, 1.5 billion people still live in an absolute poverty that is dehumanising for those who suffer it and for those of us who accept it as a fact of life. My hope and belief is that an independent Scotland will join other small countries such as Norway in becoming a global leader of a new type of development which seeks out the poorest and fosters programmes which are holistic and put the dignity of the human person at its core.

For some Scottish politicians who have gained prestige from the Union, Scotland has no distinct place on the global stage. Former Secretary General of NATO, Lord Robertson of Port Ellen, wrote in an article in 'The Scottish Review' in April 2014 that, in travelling the world with his job, 'universally and unanimously people say they don't want Britain to break up' and that in a world of geopolitical turmoil, from the Middle East to the Democratic Republic of Congo, 'Britain is one country to which the international community turns for reassurance'. Towards the end of his piece, he states that 'the world outside Scotland cares about the decision we are about to take'.

1 Lister, R. (2004) *Poverty*, Cambridge: Polity Press

WHY NOT?

Like Lord Robertson, I was the Secretary General of a large, international organisation, in my case *Caritas Internationalis*, the Confederation of 165 national Catholic aid, development and social service agencies, sometimes called the 'United Nations of Compassion'. It is probably the world's largest NGO aid and development network, using the resources of the Catholic Church for the good of all and collectively has an income of ca. $6 billion per annum. SCIAF (Scottish Catholic International Aid Fund) is the Scottish member.

I also travelled widely in the world but met very different people from Lord Robertson. Most people I met were the poor, the dispossessed, the marginalised and those trying to serve them. They were often people suffering from poverty and violence dating back to the way British imperialists – among them, sadly, Scots – shaped the modern world. They have a very different view of the independence referendum from that mentioned by Lord Robertson and the reasons are clear.

Just to take one historical example, economics Professor William Easterly of New York University[2] tells the story of one British diplomat, Sir Mark Sykes, whose shenanigans at the decolonisation of the Middle East caused a chaos which has had a hugely damaging effect on today's world.

In 1915, Sykes, on behalf of the British Government, told the Arabs that he would recognise their independence in all the territories except West Syria (today's Lebanon) which was under French influence. A year later, Sykes met French diplomats and promised them northern Palestine, the south would remain British and central Palestine, including Jerusalem, would remain an 'Allied condominium' shared by the British and the French.

Another year later, the same Sykes talked to Zionist leaders and said that in return for their support in World War I, the British would recognise Palestine as a Jewish state. Sir Mark Sykes, acting on behalf of the British Government, is responsible for the plight of the Palestinian people today, a wound that has spawned terrorism in the 21st century but whose origins are found in the decolonisation process.

Let me cite a more contemporary example of how British colonialism

---

2 Easterley, W.(2006), *The White Man's Burden: why the West's efforts to aid the rest have done so much ill and so little good*, London: Penguin Books.

impoverished former colonies by engendering conflict. In early 2014, as I have done for the previous five years, I was on the Thai side of the border with Burma where I was teaching a course in international development to Burmese refugee students on behalf of Australian Catholic University for which I worked until December 2013. They became refugees as a result of a bitter war between the Karen people and the Burmese military. In exchange for Karen assistance in fighting the Japanese, the British Government promised autonomy to the Karen but, on granting independence to Burma, broke its word and what was to be the world's longest-running civil war started. In talking to the Karen National Union's Foreign Minister who is also involved in the peace talks with the Burmese government, he was only too aware of British treachery at the time of independence and expressed a genuine interest in the workings of the Scottish Parliament and offered his good wishes for a YES vote on 18 September 2014.

I would suggest that Lord Robertson's statement that the 'one country to which the international community turns for reassurance' is Britain is delusional. For the ethnic groups of Burma or the Palestinians or many others whose current woes stem from British colonialism, the UK would be their last port of call when seeking help.

In October 2013, I was doing research among dirt-poor rural communities in Oecussi, the enclave belonging to Timor Leste (East Timor) but surrounded on the land side by Indonesia. I asked people if they would like to be part of a greater whole again, especially as Indonesia was now one of the rising economic giants of South-east Asia. They looked astonished and laughed at the absurdity of it. They talked with pride of their voting 78.5% for independence in their 'Popular Consultation' supervised by the UN but under intimidation from Indonesia. After the result, Indonesian militias went on a killing spree murdering 1,500 people. The Timorese said, 'The Scots at least can vote in safety for their independence'.

As for 'universally and unanimously, people say they don't want Britain to break up', if by 'people' Lord Robertson means the bankers who caused the global financial crisis or the IMF economists who, with structural adjustment programmes, forced developing countries to cut food subsidies, free education and health care to pay back debts to the rich, then perhaps but my wandering the world working for the poor meets with a different reaction. The world outside Scotland does indeed care about the decision we are about to take but, contrary to Lord Robertson's view, the world's people, especially the poor and the dispossessed and those who have had to struggle far more than the Scots for their independence, will welcome a Scotland shorn of British imperialist pretensions with open arms.

I cite these examples from the past because imperialism and the decolonisation process are largely the root causes of the extent of global poverty today and neo-colonialism still exists in various guises – even dressed up as aid. By becoming independent, Scotland will distance itself from this colonialist past and begin on a fresh journey to respond to the poorest of our world in a different way which listens to their real needs, maintains their dignity and leads to the flourishing of their communities not just their partial enrichment.

So, how can an independent Scotland contribute to global solidarity with the poor?

NIDOS, the Network of International Development Organisations in Scotland, published in 2013 a contribution to the independence debate – *Scotland's Place in Building a Just World*.[3] It calls for more coherent policy and practice with all government departments cooperating on building a more just world; promoting a new economy which supports socio-economic benefits over narrow fiscal growth; more equitable trade rules; more, and more innovative, aid; and climate justice. I admire the attempts by the Scottish Parliament, led by our able Scottish-Pakistani Muslim Foreign and Development Minister, Humza Yousaf, with a very limited budget to focus on a select group of the poorest countries overseas and to support development education centres at home. Aid agencies carry on campaigns nowadays rather than development education which teaches children in schools about what true development is and thus creates a generation of global citizens and well-informed voters who will be advocates for issues concerning global poverty such as why promises to the poor of the world were not kept – for example, in reaching 0.7% of Gross National Income (GNI) on aid.

3   NIDOS (2013) Scotland's Place in Building a Just World available at www.nidos.org.uk/news/scotland's-place-building-just-world.

It is significant that most of the countries which have achieved this target are in Scandinavia where there is a powerful movement among the people for supporting aid and development. For them at election time, it is an important and vote-winning topic. In *Scotland's Future*[4] the commitment to 0.7% would be enshrined in legislation (a pledge dropped by the Westminster government this year) which means that a commitment that was given in 1970 by most so-called developed countries would no longer be a political football but a pledge to humanity. In Australia, where there was bipartisan support for reaching 0.5% of GNI for aid by 2015 has now been forgotten by the new neo-liberal conservative Coalition government and it was drastically reduced, making the commitment of Australia, the so-called 'lucky country', to the global poor a farce.

Another important commitment in *Scotland's Future* is a pledge to relieve the poorest countries of debt. This will release funds for social and educational programmes in developing countries. After NGO lobbying in the 1990s, Tanzania spent its debt relief on abolishing school fees which saw a 66% increase in school attendance; Mozambique spent it on free immunisations for children against preventable diseases and Uganda spent it on giving access to clean water for 2.2 million people.

Another commitment is the implementation of the 'do no harm' principle in development by only supporting NGO projects which do not make people dependent on them and do good for communities which requires that projects be sustainable and holistic. There is a commitment to link climate change with development and not allowing commercial and other considerations to influence the approach. The UK used to receive, as policy, 70% of its aid budget back because governments of both hues insisted on the beneficiary using British goods and services. Although the current aid budget is officially untied, of 117 major aid contracts recently undertaken by the UK Department of International Development (DFID) worth $750 million, only 9 are non-UK firms, thus depriving engineers and designers in developing countries of employment.

There is a commitment in *Scotland's Future* to fulfilling the obligations

4   Scottish Government (2013) Scotland's Future: your guide to an independent Scotland available from www.scotreferendum.com.

of the Millennium Development Goals (MGDs) which are the nearest instrument we have internationally to reducing global poverty. Many so-called developed countries have not done their part in Goal 8 – Global Partnership – by providing the money to pay for the other seven such as reducing poverty by half and aiming for universal primary education. The new post-2015 framework of MDGs is being worked on by the Open Working Group on Sustainable Development Goals set up at the Rio+20 Conference in 2012. This aims to unite ending global poverty with sustainable development needs but has to be less Western in terms of design and timeframe, and needs to stop focusing on an interpretation of poverty that stresses inadequate socio-economic outcomes. Poverty is multi-dimensional and any new plan must integrate the social, economic, political, cultural and religious dimensions.

The dignity of the human person has to be at the centre of any development strategy and that requires an ethical approach to development. Government strategies are more concerned with economic growth than human transformation. They tend to support large infrastructural aid projects which do not benefit the poorest. China, in its 'development' policy for Pacific Islands, even builds barracks for soldiers out of the aid budget. James Wolfensohn, former head of the World Bank, admitted that it was the top 40% of society which benefited from their projects. We need a strategy focused on the poorest and I believe that we are more likely to make this shift in an independent Scotland with social democratic credentials rather than in a UKIP-tainted, xenophobic UK.

Denis Goulet (1931–2006), the father of development ethics condensed his thought in three ethical goals with three ethical strategies. The goals were (a) life sustenance (the importance of life-sustaining goods such as food, shelter, medicine etc), (b) esteem – the need for all of us regardless of culture, for respect, dignity and recognition, even as societies become more materially wealthy and (c) freedom. The Nobel Prize-winner for Economics in 1998, Amartya Sen, has taken up this link with development and freedom by perceiving the expansion of freedom as both the primary end and the main means of development. To do that, we must rid society of 'unfreedoms' such as a lack of education, lack of income and a lack of access to health care.

The first of the three ethical strategies was about an *abundance of goods* – people have to have enough to be more – to have a good life. He talked of how too much wealth in a context of poverty leads to a dehumanisation of life for both rich and poor and how extreme consumption can result in a distortion of the 'good life' – that it is about the accumulation of wealth ('having more') rather than being successful or doing something valuable ('being more').

The second strategy was called *universal solidarity*. People must appreciate a common human-ness in the human family and go beyond differences of race, ethnicity and language. We all share a common destiny on the planet and therefore should care for it together. In other words, the individual want comes second to the overwhelming common good, the good of all society but particularly of the poorest in that society. In an individualistic society, that is very difficult to achieve but is a pre-requisite to any form of ethical development. To achieve this, which goes against central tenets of neo-liberal capitalism, it is necessary to recast social relations and institutions and make them serve societies where equality is core.

The third strategy was *participation*. The poor should become receivers of development and also the agents of their destiny. In Amartya Sen's words, they become the 'doers' of any development project and the 'judges' of the outcomes of the project, not the 'beneficiaries'. This kind of participation also lessens the power of elites, those who hold power, whether in a refugee camp or a village, and shares that power with people who have never had it before.

So what do these theoretical discussions have to do with the lives of the people we are interested in – the poor and the vulnerable, especially in so-called developing countries?

In October 2013, I made a research trip to Cambodia to look at projects which applied ethics to development. The projects were organised by a Cambodian NGO with an Australian partner. They followed the kind of ethical development which can be termed a 'dignity-based approach' as it puts the dignity of the person at the centre rather than economic growth. They sought out the poorest, the disabled and destitute or those who were HIV positive and built programs around them. By focusing on them, they sent out ripples to the wider community whose better off members (but still poor by our standards) who had dismissed the poorest as lazy and drunkards, then began to invite them for the first time to village or commune meetings to decide about matters affecting the whole community – from irrigation to road building. In one case, a farmer who would be in the middle poor category was so impressed that he gave land to build a school for the whole community. In other words, people who had previously been shunned by mainstream society began to be accepted as full members of the community.

Through participative training programmes which taught respect between men and women and set up self-help groups, domestic violence and excessive drinking have declined. Children of illiterate parents now go to school. There has been an increase in hygiene and a decrease in disease. They have clean water, clean houses and yards and small shops and an increase in productivity such as growing vegetables to sell or consume. Before, there was a feeling of hopelessness as many of the villagers told me. Now, they had been made the subjects of their own development and not the object of someone else's idea of what it is to be developed and were lifting themselves out of a poverty which ground down their humanity. A 15 year old girl, an HIV+ orphan, told me of her dream of becoming a nurse or a doctor. Healthy, cared for and educated, she may now realise her dream. This is development as transformation – the transformation of becoming more fully human, of realising your capabilities, of becoming free because the 'unfreedoms' such as a lack of confidence, education and a sense of belonging to a community have been addressed.

This is called good community development. It is people-centred, needs-based, rights-based, and holistic and takes into account all aspects of a community's life. It is also based on their dignity as human beings. Yet so few Governments follow this approach.

I believe that Scotland, with its history as a communitarian society and a concern for the poor at home and overseas, will vote for an independent Government which takes this people-centred approach to overseas development seriously. There are already glimpses of it in the White Paper and in the NIDOS document. What we require, as a first step, is the sovereignty to make these ideas about rolling back some of the ills of colonialism to realise a world of peace and justice in which Scotland takes a full and active part as an independent nation.

CHAPTER FOUR

Backlash: The Political Economy of Voting NO

JAMES FOLEY

SO FAR, THE QUESTION of Scotland's economic future has dominated the referendum debate. With everything staked on this one issue, nuanced accounts get little coverage next to heated polemics and propaganda; and far from facilitating calm discussion, journalists encourage pointless confrontations between the two sides.

Nationalists rarely admit the hazards facing a new Scottish economy for fear of emboldening the Unionist campaign. As a result, boosterism and unthinking optimism dominates their communications strategy. In a recent example, Alex Salmond boasted that the average Scot would net a windfall of £1,000 if they voted YES, and that Scotland would be one of the world's richest countries. The first minister conveniently forgot to mention that a large part of profit disappears overseas.

That same week, mirroring Salmond, Danny Alexander claimed Scots would net £1,400 if they stayed loyal to the Union. The calculations were equally misleading. So too was the Treasury claim that a new Scottish state would face start-up costs of £2.7 billion. Their own authority, Professor Dunleavy, downgraded the figure to £200 million, and scolded the Treasury for combining 'ludicrous' calculations with 'crude misinformation'. Both sides share the blame for trivialising the debate on the economy. But while the media interrogate the sillier claims of the SNP and Scottish officials, those of the Treasury and Better Together receive only cursory scrutiny. According to Professor John Robertson of the University of West of Scotland, press and broadcast journalism show 'undue deference to the apolitical wisdom' of London think tanks, and treats '[UK] Treasury officials... as detached academic figures to be trusted.'

Although journalists dutifully relay YES Scotland's and Better Together's press statements, their framing of the debate implies bias. It favours continuity, since they fixate on the risks of separation while ignoring the risks of union. This reflects, as Robertson argued, an editorial deference towards UK institutions. Trusting in the wisdom and neutrality the British state and its mandarins, Scotland's media consider the stability of Britain and its neoliberal economics beyond reproach. And despite the rise of UKIP and a likely referendum on EU membership, no think tank measures the cost to Scotland of Britain's many political crises. These conformist prejudices are entrenched in the debate.

But I want to pose a problem that the media generally avoid: the dangers of a NO vote. It draws on an ominous precedent, since, prior to the 1979 referendum, Scotland's Unionist press was equally unwilling to quantify the dangers of staying still. 'How much of Scotland's economy will be left intact if a Scottish Assembly gets the go-ahead on March 1?' demanded an *Express* editorial in the late 1970s. 'Will our coal mines go gaily on? Will Ravenscraig or Linwood thrive? Will Bathgate flourish and Dounreay prosper?' Fearing the economic costs of change, Scotland voted (if not overall, then at least in sufficient numbers) to stick with British institutions. As a result, there was little defence against Mrs Thatcher's monetarist blitzkrieg, and Scotland lost many native industries, devastating communities for generations. The lesson today is simple: you can't vote to keep capitalism static. Change is unavoidable, and the real question must be: whose politics will command change?

An Insecure Public Sector

Whichever way Scotland votes, political conflicts will shape its economic future. Journalists have queried how political hazards, such as doubts over EU admission or confusion over Sterling's future, could limit Scotland's policy options – but what certainties does a NO vote offer?

Since the 1970s, Scottish living standards have just about kept pace with the UK average, despite Scotland having lost key industries. There are several reasons for this, including emigration, inward investment, and two decades of deregulated finance. But, above all, it's because Scotland's public sector has plugged the gaps left by a laggard capitalist economy. Overall, Scottish public expenditure is about 10% per person higher than the UK average.

For critics, this proves Scotland's status as a 'privileged subsidy junky'. But the real story is far more complex. For generations, the UK has devoted its monetary and fiscal policies to feeding the growth of global finance in London. Reflecting these priorities, the City and its surrounding commuter areas 'overheat', while ex-manufacturing peripheries decline. Government spending often reinforces this. Thatcher's government, for instance, splurged billions on capital projects like the M25, the Docklands light railway, and new terminals at Heathrow and Gatwick. Privatisation of public industries also profited London's financial district at the expense of so-called 'peripheral' regions. Today, projects like HS2 will further centralise Britain's economy. London's overwhelming role reflects more than unfettered free markets; it also reflects the state's enabling role in promoting them.

Higher spending in areas such as Scotland thus masks the hidden costs of economic policies designed to feed London's growth. Rather than engage in economic planning, the UK has institutionalised 'fiscal transfers' to balance the inevitable tensions that arise from uneven development. Scotland's ostensible 'privileges' rest on two interconnected problems. One is the political threat posed by nationalism; the other is North Sea oil's long-term significance to Britain's balance of payments.

Whether Scotland actually benefits from these arrangements is questionable. Between 1976 and 2006, following the discovery of oil and the establishment of the Barnett formula, Scotland's economy grew at an annual average 1.8%. This compares poorly to a UK average of 2.3%, as well as to similar European economies such as Ireland (5.4%), Iceland (3.4%), Norway (3.1%), Finland (2.9%), Austria (2.4%) and Sweden (2.3%). Given that only Norway enjoyed a parallel oil boom in the oil, these figures should alarm Unionists and nationalists alike.

Scotland's share of UK spending rests on *conventions*, not *law*, and no account of economic risks should ignore this. Public spending is negotiable when circumstances change, a threat which causes Scottish officials to behave like compliant Westminster mandarins. And for conservatives

Britain-wide, the so-called Barnett Formula which underpins Scotland's public spending, and thus its most secure jobs, is a persistent grievance.

Scotland's 'right' to higher spending ultimately rests on its ability to make trouble. If the threat of independence disappears, it will embolden parties like UKIP and the Tory Eurosceptic right – as well as Labour opportunists in English constituencies – seeking to revise Scotland's share. Academic experts have already expressed this view to MSPs in Holyrood. Professor David Heald of Aberdeen University told Scottish leaders to expect 'big pressure post-referendum, in the case of a 'NO' vote, for a review of Barnett'. He added that a review would likely mean 'cutting Scotland's public expenditure', due to grievances about Scotland's supposed overfunding.

The political economy of Westminster will reinforce these pressures. For generations, New Labour and the Tories have competed to please 'swing voters' concentrated in middle England constituencies. Scots' views make little impact on electoral calculations, since everyone broadly expects them to return Labour candidates. Nonetheless, devolution and the threat of nationalism largely kept Scotland's spending beyond the reaches of the anti-Barnett crusaders. If Scotland votes NO, Westminster parties will face the added pressure of a rising UKIP-Tory Eurosceptic power bloc; and with austerity forecast to last for at least a decade, convenient scapegoats will be sought. All the signs point to backlash against Scotland. With limited political defences, and Holyrood neutered of its principle threat (independence), the rising right-wing power bloc will aim to strip Scotland of its 'privileged' spending priorities.

While this scenario I, of course, hypothetical, it's considerably more realistic than the doom-laden independence scenarios painted by Better Together. Whether in the form of an unfavourable 'devo plus' package, or in the form of an outright attack on Scottish institutions, the axe dangles above Scotland's public sector. If we vote NO, can we trust Westminster to reward our loyalty? They didn't in 1979. Westminster's attention will focus on the political conflicts of the South East, principally Europe and immigration. With limited choices to appease the right, the likelihood is a squeeze on Scottish 'privilege', and deeper cuts.

The Certainty of Tory Rule

It is 59 years since Scotland returned a Tory majority. Nonetheless, we have endured Conservative rule at Westminster for more than half the time since. The economic damage of those years is almost incalculable.

If Scotland votes YES, neither a Tory government nor a Tory opposition at Holyrood is foreseeable. Instead, the SNP and Labour will compete for power. By contrast, based on current electoral trends, we can probably expect Conservative rule at Westminster for one out of every two parliaments at Westminster. While Holyrood will hold some autonomy, Thatcher or Cameron-style governments in London will set Scotland's agenda. As mentioned earlier, they will aim to limit the scope for populist pro-welfare policies (in Scotland and elsewhere).

This will exercise a twofold drag on effective Labour governments. From historical experience, we know that Conservative oppositions are permanent blocs aiming to roll back the best Labour reforms. Their existence threatens every part of public provision. Thus, small bits of progress under Westminster Labour – from the NHS and council housing to now-forgotten Blairite successes like Sure Start – are always exposed to cuts in later parliaments. By contrast, the SNP often resists privatisation from a position to the left of Labour. Although the nationalists are by no means a consistent social democratic opposition, they are not outright capitalists either; in socio-economic terms, their base is similar to Labour's.

Another problem is that Westminster's voting structure forces Labour to compete for reactionary swing constituencies. This explains why, in defiance of all logic and evidence, Labour politicians continue to scapegoat benefit claimants and immigrants for endemic economic problems. Since Labour enforces 'party unity' UK-wide, its Scottish leadership has found itself defending unpopular policies to keep Westminster backbenchers happy.

Yet despite Blair's and Brown's willing surrender to global business, the worst Labour governments are always better than the best Tory administrations. What would the last 59 years of Scottish politics look like with no Conservative governments, and no Conservative oppositions? Given the worldwide trends of privatisation and market-domination, it's impossible to believe Scotland would have become an isolated socialist paradise.

But retention of serious industries and quality jobs would have been a national priority. Our public institutions would be stronger. And trade unionists would be free to organise, whereas under UK legislation, they are the most throttled in Europe (barring Lithuania).

Looking forward, to the next 59 years, what damage will further Tory governments do to Scotland's economy and society? And how can we best resist it? Only a vote for independence gives Labour or equivalent parties a realistic chance to rebuild the base of social democracy. While capitalism will always corrupt electoral politics, at least they would be open to influence and public pressure. Tory governments, by contrast, manage without democratic scrutiny, ruling in the name of big finance and landed property.

The Neoliberal Model

Westminster's main parties, its civil servants, and its service ecosystem of think tanks and journalists are intent on saving the neoliberal model. This means further doses of austerity, privatisation, and deregulation for an indefinite future. Voting NO locks Scotland into this model. Based on current trends, this allows us to make certain judgements about our immediate prospects.

The obvious impact will be rising inequality, far beyond what we've already seen. Britain has already become one of the developed world's most unequal societies, with enormous divisions of wealth and income. There's a danger that we become ambivalent to the moral effects of an economy that actively promotes homelessness, low wages, and child poverty. Nonetheless, since these issues are covered elsewhere in this volume, we will address other, hidden dangers.

Besides inequality, Britain's free market approach means persistent low investment, financial speculation, and precarious jobs. A nation's commitment to research and investment is hugely significant, because it is the main means by which capitalist economies can improve social conditions while overall profits rise. Without it, growth will largely depend on low wages. A staggering feature of Britain's present economic order is the low rate of investment. Out of 173 countries (including sub-Saharan Africa), only 13 invest less than the UK. The main reason for this is an institutionalised preference in British economics for short-term profitability, the proverbial fast buck. Britain can prosper without investment, for a while. But its wealth will depend on further bubbles of deregulated finance – and the result will be ever-riskier investments, driven by an ever-shadier boom and bonus culture. It takes little imagination to forecast the outcome: the UK will enter new rounds of unsustainable windfalls and harsher crises; and as with 2008, vulnerable groups will suffer most.

The so-called UK economic recovery proves these trends. Look beyond the official GDP figures and the evidence is there: property speculation is covering for low business investment, the short-term for the long-term. A third feature of UK economics, the growth of so-called self-employment, is not some new entrepreneurial boom. Instead, it represents an explosion of insecure work driven by the persistent unwillingness of businesses to invest, allied to government schemes to bully vulnerable people off benefits and into, no matter how low-paid or menial. This is a foretaste of Britain's economic future.

'The United Kingdom has a malfunctioning economy, vast liabilities and is close to going broke,' notes *Guardian* economics editor Larry Elliott. The present crisis has reinforced Britain's tradition of underinvestment, financial adventurism, and inequality, and under Westminster, Labour has few alternatives. By contrast, Scotland's anti-Conservative consensus, although far from perfect, presents the best opportunity for a new social consensus.

Conclusion

Both sides of the referendum debate are guilty of fantasy economics. The SNP and YES Scotland trade in empty optimism about Scotland's prosperity, as if goodwill alone can overcome the overlapping crises of contemporary capitalism. By contrast, Better Together's prophecies of doom and bullying tactics have discredited what passes for British democracy. Even if they defeat the YES movement, their real victim will be the Scottish Labour Party, who will be culpable for the backlash if Scotland votes NO.

Curiously, no part of mainstream Scotland has openly reckoned with the dangers of a NO vote. The scenarios described in this chapter, it must be admitted, are often social and political rather than crudely economic. But equally, whether an independent Scotland secures its place in the EU is a political decision, as is Westminster's attitude to a currency union. If they vote no, Scots guarantee themselves Tory rule and a submissive Labour Party; a precarious public sector as Britain agonises over Europe and immigration; and proximity to London's reckless, finance-led growth machine. The political, moral, and economic effects will be very real and very damaging.

Remaining loyal to British institutions is thus a recipe for permanent crisis. The paltry costs of establishing new Scottish institutions – estimated at £200 million initially, followed by £900 million down the line – should be understood in this context. Measured against the costs of staying in the UK, these start-up costs amount to prudent investments in a more secure future.

Unionists insist that Scotland should endure the austerity backlash in solidarity with vulnerable communities elsewhere in the UK. Nobody should ignore this serious moral argument. But again, Scotland can offer one of only two gifts to Britain. One is an extra 40-or-so Labour MPs to join the Westminster cohort every four years. The other is a social democratic experiment to the North, freed from the fetters of Toryism, which will give a little breathing room for social investment, solidarity, and planning. For those who believe Labour still offers hope, the choice should be simple.

CHAPTER FIVE

The Meaning of Things

ROBIN MCALPINE

WHAT IS THE DIFFERENCE between sheep and mutton? This question was put to a lecture theatre full of students by the man generally considered the father of semiotics, Ferdinand de Saussure. His point is simple – in English a sheep is a living thing that runs about fields and mutton is dead material that you eat, while in French 'mutton' is the same word for both things (in the way that in English we now use 'lamb' to mean both things). Is living lamb and dead lamb the same thing? Is a French sheep fundamentally different from an English sheep, either living or dead?

This is the starting point of the whole field of semiology. Saussure argues against the idea that (with apologies for all the inverted commas) 'words' 'name' 'things'. The prevailing idea had been that 'things' are definite, objective and exist independent of any linguistic context and that 'words' are 'objects' which are also fixed and in a fixed relationship with the 'things' they describe. Except, where does snow turn into slush and when does slush turn back into snow? Ten people looking at the same 'thing' would all pick a different moment of thaw to change the naming word from 'snow' to 'slush'. What Saussure is arguing is that there are 'signifiers' (in this case, words) which link to something that is 'signified' (in this case objects). It's just that the relationship isn't fixed but constantly changing. And – crucially – the words change the thing just as much as the words change as the thing changes.

What is Labour? There are few abstract concepts in Scottish life which are simultaneously so hard to pin down and yet so widely understood. There is the 'Labour Party', but that is not really taken to be what 'Labour in Scotland' means. The concept is much wider and contains within it 'Labour communities', 'Labour voters', the 'Labour movement' and much more. It is here that the problems really begin. Lots of 'Labour communities' have not been voting Labour for coming on a decade now. A high proportion of what are generally called 'Labour voters' don't actually vote. The 'Labour movement' is now mainly taken to mean the Labour Party and the trade unions. But few in the trade unions are now loyal to Labour. In Unite (the biggest donor to the Labour Party) the number of its members voting Labour is close to being matched by the number of its members voting SNP. Many also vote Green or SSP.

And the political party itself? Well 'Scottish Labour' is only a trading name of the British Labour Party so there isn't really a *Scottish* Labour *Party* (certainly not in terms of a separate membership or governance structure). This in turn means that it isn't clear how many members Labour has in Scotland. I heard the number 5,000 suggested. It seemed low even to me. Then the Falkirk selection wrangle came along and it turned out that in the heart of Labour-supporting Scotland there were little more than 100 members. In that light 5,000 across Scotland doesn't look as unlikely as it first seemed. Is this what 'Labour' has become? A voter that doesn't vote in a community that has moved on from a movement that has largely turned its back on a political party that is barely there?

And yet we all know exactly what we mean by 'Labour Scotland' – and if anything there are signs that it is growing stronger rather than weaker. 'Labour Scotland' has become a state of mind, often unlinked to the party. At a meeting of the Scottish Independence Convention around the time the first details of the referendum were emerging, I recall noting that of about 20 people round the table all but two had been in the Labour Party and most still described themselves as 'Labour people', 'of the Labour movement' or as some other form of Labour identifier. It is not just in the independence campaign but almost constantly since Blair and Labour's involvement in the Iraq War that 'Labour Buts' have become seemingly omnipresent. As in 'I'm Labour but...'

Is 'Labour Scotland' really growing stronger? Yes, I believe it is. We've been told that social attitude surveys show the UK has become more right-wing in recent years. But I think this is a misreading. I believe that if you look at attitudes since 2008 what you will find is an almost universal ramping up of anger. People generally are just angry about the string of failures which started with Iraq, ran through the financial crash, the political corruption scandal, the media corruption scandal and five years of austerity. They feel the pain, they know that this was done by an elite but they know the elite are not suffering. So, yes, they're generally angry. It's just that social attitude surveys tend to ask people to make more value judgements about the poor (should welfare be cut?) than about the rich (should the super-rich pay substantially more tax?).

Anger is like a shockwave that seeks routes of outlet. In England much of this shockwave has released itself through UKIP. But in Scotland (despite a single BBC-induced UKIP victory) it has not really sought an outlet to the right. Not for the first time in recent Scottish political history, a vote which largely punished the political right has been dissected for evidence that, somewhere underneath all the left posturing, Scottish voters aren't *really* all that left-wing.

In Scotland there is an entirely different outlet for anger – the independence movement. And it is here that we find 'Labour Scotland' alive and thriving. It's just that this part of 'Labour Scotland' widely detests the Labour Party. They exist everywhere from Labour for Independence through the Radical Independence Campaign to the very active trade union presence in YES and perhaps above all the vast array of 'unaligned' campaigners who all claim to be from a Labour background (and you're as likely to find them in Business for Scotland as in Women for Independence or National Collective). They almost never get through a speech without saying 'I'm voting YES so we can have a real Labour government'.

Of course, they don't mean that – or at least not in capital letters. One indisputable fact of the campaign is that it has polarised the views of many active campaigners. A universal constant not much less reliable than the speed of light is that left-of-centre independence supporters really, really dislike the current Scottish Labour Party. It's not like Labour hasn't given them reason, by joining a coalition in which they are the only group which isn't absolutely unequivocally right wing. But it's really the vitriolic personal attacks that have come from Scottish Labour towards left-of-centre independence supporters which have done the most damage, along with a narrative which is hard to believe. Until you've heard a Labour MSP tell a room full of trade union activists in a working class town hall that Scotland's socialist traditions are a myth you may not have properly understood the dynamic of the independence campaign.

It is an unfortunate position for Scottish Labour to get into. On the opposite shore the independence campaign is mainly a left-wing grassroots affair, seeing independence as the only alternative to the right-wing-and-getting-worse nature of Westminster rule. Behind Labour London is responding to the same pressures by drifting to the right and using more and more dog-whistle tactics on immigration and welfare. Beside it is a Tory-Lib Dem coalition, the Orange Order, millionaire land owners and the entire British establishment. In the logic of this campaign its only route forward is into a sea of isolation and confusion. Scottish Labour has dived in. The Labour Party in the UK now talks about being harder on welfare and being kinder on welfare at the same time but in different places. If it wasn't for the protection of the *Daily Mail* and the other Unionist newspapers, it is hard to see how this dissonance could be credibly sustained.

Indeed, it is generally hard to see how Labour could have avoided some sort of implosion during this campaign if it wasn't for the wholehearted support of a pro-union media which knows that whether it supports Labour or not, only Labour has a real chance of bringing out enough NO voters. The performances of Johann Lamont, Anas Sarwar and Margaret Curran have been poor by anyone's standards. Lamont in particular is a woeful performer, unable to judge the right tone or pitch in most circumstances and the most gaffe-prone political leader I can remember. Senior Labour figures will openly tell you in private that they know there is zero chance of Labour winning a Scottish election under Johann Lamont. In the long term I doubt the media is doing Labour any favours by facilitating complete denial about its true performance.

I continue to believe (against the mainstream narrative) that the SNP victory in 2011 was in significant part the result of tactical voting against Scottish Labour. This tactical vote seems to me to have come from two sources. First, the disillusioned left which wishes to see Labour punished severely for its actions since 2003. And second, a wider community which recognises Labour's behaviour as being that of an 'old power' which is fighting not for principle but for its own privilege. Labour never accepted its defeat in 2007 and remained convinced of its own entitlement. And we all noticed.

What the independence campaign has really done is to take the two-dimensionality of normal knockabout party politics and plunge it into three dimensions by creating a space which has been populated by political people who are not in political parties. The mainstream media continues to present the whole affair as Punch and Judy –Scottish Labour against the SNP. This is wrong. In fact the campaign is largely 'Labour' against Westminster – if you accept the wider and more inclusive definition of Labour.

What cannot be in doubt is that if you take away the badges and the branding, ignore the distractions and dissimulation and concentrate on the arguments, analysis and proposals, what most people understand by 'Labour' is pro-independence. Meanwhile, what people know as the Scottish Labour Party is being pulled by the logic of this campaign into fawning support for military parades, Union Jack-waving and neoliberal think tanks. Perhaps worst of all, Labour in Scotland is wedded to a political analysis which simply cannot admit the reality of the performance of the United Kingdom across a range of indicators measuring the quality of life for working people and society's most vulnerable. It certainly can't admit the truth about the UK's real economic performance.

Labour could have responded to the independence challenge in one of two ways. It could have wedded itself to a genuine shift in devolution to recognise that Scotland does vote differently and that this is a necessary pressure-valve to enable continued divergence in UK politics. Or it could have gone the opposite direction, focussing on the reform of Britain, making the whole of Britain more 'Labour' (in the wide sense) and so more like Scotland. What it did was both and neither. Even the most ardent supporters of Scottish Labour don't raise its 'Devo Nano' proposals if they can avoid it, because they know that if there is one informed person in earshot it'll be an embarrassing conversation. The devolutionary wing of the party couldn't carry the day. It is hard to see how Labour could have promised less.

Meanwhile there is a very clear move from some in Labour to centralise strategy. Many Labour figures talk about the need to 'coincide' policy and strategy on either side of the border. Andy Burnham's comments on unifying NHS policy across the UK is only the latest example. Johann Lamont spoke in similar tones when she made her 'something for nothing' intervention and Iain Davidson and Brian Wilson have both spoken in public about stripping powers from the Scottish Parliament, mainly so the SNP can never create a different policy culture in Scotland. But – crucially – this is not connected to reform of the British State. There is a widespread expectation in the Labour Party that Scotland should once again suffer like everyone else in Britain.

So in the perennial debate on Labour and Scotland, how have the signifiers and the signified changed in their relationships? The 'Labour' part, still signifying a social democratic politics rooted in working class experience and mythology, is still there and strong. The 'Labour Party' bit is still clearly there and it refers to an identifiable object. It's just that the meaning of 'Labour' and the meaning of the 'Labour Party' have diverged massively. Labour is still how we say 'social democrat' or 'socialist' in Scotland. The Labour Party is not really either of these things but it does signify an important part of the British Establishment. That, after all, is what the Labour Party really is. It is populated by members of the establishment, operates primarily in the orbit of the establishment and pursues a political programme which does not stray outside the bounds of what is acceptable (if perhaps undesirable) in the British Establishment. When it comes right down to it Tony Blair called off a fraud investigation into an arms manufacturer solely because it would embarrass members of the British establishment. Does anyone really think Ed Milliband would act differently? David Milliband certainly wouldn't have.

None of this is to explore alternatives. The SNP has been better than the Labour Party and has had more progressive policies. Then again, the SNP is now as much a part of the Scottish establishment as Labour is of the British establishment. And those more progressive policies of the SNP do look suspiciously like 'just enough to outflank Labour but no more than that'. If we accept flexibility of terminology and the changing meaning of words we might argue that Scotland is still Labour but Labour is no longer Scottish and no longer Labour. The SNP is a bit Labour but not too Labour. Or, to put it another way, while at Westminster politics has failed to live up to people's standards, in Scotland politics has failed to be the specific thing that people want.

Because in the end the one thing that Saussure did not claim is that there is no such thing as a sheep. There is definitely a woolly creature in a field grazing about. We can name it or not name it. We can agree on the name or all have our own. We can keep changing the name as many times as we like. But if we don't feed it, it will die. The Labour Party can call Scotland's social democrats and socialists 'Labour'. The SNP can claim the same people for themselves. They can all argue about what it means. But in the end social transformation is an entity that you feed or which dies. Call it what you want; Scotland wants change and Labour isn't offering it. The line between sheep and mutton is a fine one, measuring no more than a heartbeat. It is a line on which Labour in Scotland is perched. Perilously.

CHAPTER SIX

Ireland: The Real Elephant in the Room

OWEN DUDLEY EDWARDS

... and yes I said yes I will Yes.
Last words of James Joyce *Ulysses*

THE STRANGEST THING about the NO campaign is that it is fighting to retain what hasn't existed for over 200 years. When in 1603, James VI of Scotland inherited the throne of England from Elizabeth I of England, he wanted to be known as 'King of Great Britain, France and Ireland' but had to settle for being 'King of England, Scotland, France and Ireland' and it wasn't until the Union of 1707 that his great-granddaughter Queen Anne became the first ruler of Britain to be called monarch of 'Great Britain, France, and Ireland'. The 'France' bit was an assertion from 1340 to 1801, that is from Edward III to George III, although St Joan and other French leaders drove English rule from France in Henry VI's mid-15th century reign, and Mary I lost the last English foothold on continental France over a century later when the French reconquered Calais: David Cameron isn't the first English leader to become intoxicated with imaginary kingdoms...

On the first of January 1801 the Union of England and Scotland ended, and George III was styled King 'of the United Kingdom of Great Britain and Ireland'. So is strict constitutional theory what Mr Cameron calls 'the UK' when he means united England and Scotland is something that has never existed in that sense. Officially the United Kingdom 1707–1800 was 'Great Britain'. The UK began with the parliamentary union of these islands in 1801. Yet Mr Cameron and his merry men (Mr Alistair Darling, Mr Nicholas Clegg, Mr George Osborne, Mr Alistair Carmichael, and their disowned prodigal son Mr Nigel Farage, etc etc) hear no Ireland, see no Ireland, speak no Ireland.

That United Kingdom actually came to an end in 1922 but protocol only recognised the new situation at the present Queen Elizabeth's coronation when she was styled Queen 'of the United Kingdom of Great Britain and Northern Ireland'.

History seems to live on a diet of ironies. No ruler of the UK of Great Britain and Ireland ever won such popularity in what is now the Republic of Ireland as Queen Elizabeth on her visit there. Her magnanimity, her wisdom, her sense of comedy, and her beautiful intonation of the Irish Language made her a hero to those who were not her subjects. She also advised all of us to bow to the past but not be bound by it.

The NO-men seem incapable of taking her advice.

The two Unions – Ireland, Scotland and the Survival of the United Kingdom (2012) is a splendid discussion of the two Unions by Edinburgh's Sir Richard Lodge Professor of History, Alvin Jackson, and it very properly begins with a quotation from what Mr David Cameron has told us is his favourite history book, H.E. Marshall's *Our Island Story* (1905): *You know that England, Ireland, Scotland and Wales are all joined together. The first two to be joined together were England and Ireland.*

Since the book means so much to Mr Cameron, it's a pity he doesn't remember it better, or reread it, and the emphasis in this sentence deserves his attention. The Union of Great Britain and Ireland, and of Scotland and England, are not the reality of their relationships. These Acts of Union were both administrative conveniences (a useful word, 'convenience'), primarily for purposes of whatever war England was waging at that time, the War of the Spanish Succession in 1707, the Napoleonic Wars in 1800–01. Our lives together have been going on much longer, often divided internally, often at odds with one another, occasionally conquered one by one, as England, Wales, Ireland, and Scotland were all conquered by Oliver Cromwell who then declared us all united, and summoned us all to his attempts at Parliaments (which however proved an administrative inconvenience) after he had killed a sufficient number of us (at Naseby, Drogheda, Wexford, Dunbar, etc). Cromwell united us, if not for him, then against him. And over the centuries, we've all had to deal with other tough nuts (the nuttiness frequently being even greater than the toughness). Edward I was a horror in his dealings with Wales and Scotland, but Ireland owes him a deep debt: he gave it its first Parliament and thus, however unintentionally, founded representative government whence came democracy in Ireland.

The British-Irish UK Parliament reached its high point in the 19th century when its development of mass constitutional pressure groups under Daniel O'Connell, agrarian revolt, party manoeuvre, tactics and strategy under Charles Stewart Parnell, helped democratise the politics of our islands. Mr Cameron and friends may be right to claim the Union as the nest or nurse of democracy, liberty, statesmanship, &c, but it wasn't under the Union he thinks he is saving. It was under the one abolished in 1922, abolition affirmed in 1952.

Dr Gordon Brown in recent years while apparently on a voyage to discover where on earth is Britain, complains that Scottish independence would make 'foreigners' of those Scots resident in England. It's a nasty word, 'foreigner', as in:

> A foolish young driver named Warrener was severely told off by the coroner, when he ran down a Dame at the end of our lane: what a fuss to make over a foreigner!

Mr Cameron is ready enough to plead heartbreak, or to imply all Scots secretly agree with him or to proclaim their identity in lusting for bigger and better bombs and other weapons of mass destruction, but he sings a little softly as to the charge of Scots in England becoming foreigners to Scots in Scotland. With his name, it's natural we should look at his case. And it seems quite natural that he should remember his Cameron ancestors in, for instance, the fervent hero-worship accorded the most famous Cameron by Macaulay, regardless of Macaulay's being a Whig and Cameron of Lochiel being a Jacobite:

> He was a gracious master, a trusty ally, a terrible enemy. His countenance and bearing were singularly noble. He had repeatedly been victorious in single combat. He was a hunter of great fame. He made vigorous war on the wolves which, down to his time, preyed on the red deer of the Grampians; and by his hand perished the last of the ferocious breed which is known to have wandered at large in our

island. Nor was Lochiel less distinguished by intellectual than by bodily vigour. He might indeed have seemed ignorant to educated and travelled Englishmen, who had studied the classics under Busby at Westminster and under Aldrich at Oxford, who had learned something about the sciences among Fellows of the Royal Society, and something about the fine arts in the galleries of Florence and Rome. But though Lochiel had very little knowledge of books, he was eminently wise in council, eloquent in debate, ready in devising expedients, and skilful in managing the minds of men.

And Macaulay goes on to see Lochiel's character forecast by Homer in *Odysseus*. Now if anyone whom you and I could claim as ancestor had been described like that, however modest in ourselves and ready to admit that we might disagree with our ancestors about much, surely we would get a thrill about the relationship however secret. Perhaps Mr Cameron (leaving out the last wolf) might feel a little diminished by the association. To have his best known feat of horsemanship going out riding with Rebekah Wade may not quite equate him with a 'hunter of great fame'. His wisdom in council, his eloquence in debate, his readiness in expedients, his skill in mind management might look a little tawdry by comparison with Lochiel's. And no doubt bawling schoolboy ruderies supported by followers emitting noises of animal resonance in the House of Commons withers in contrast to the charge of the Camerons at Killicrankie when in Macaulay's words:

> It was long remembered in Lochaber than Lochiel took off what probably was the only pair of shoes in his clan, and charged barefoot at the head of his men... in two minutes the battle was lost and won.

True, Macanlay while a Whig, was the son of a Gaelic speaking Highlander, and one with the wit to add local folklore to his documents and broadsides in research. True, he was so far enthralled by his own narratives as to forget what side he thought he was on at Killiecrankie. But Mr Cameron, for all that he says Scotland voting YES would break his heart, cannot summon the thought of a shoe or a foot of Lochiel to his aid. Within moments of his prognosis of cardiac rupture, he was calling Mr Alex Salmond 'Alex the Unready'. He is so deeply deScottified, so far as a foreigner, so abroad an alien, that he must needs fall back on Anglo-

Saxon history to find appropriate abuse when performing at Perth on Thursday 3 July 2014. And he clearly assumed his audience of Scottish Tories as ill-equipped in Scottish history as himself, while being readily familiar with Ethelred the Unready King of England (978–1016, exiled when Swegn Forkbeard conquered England – is it this which makes Mr Cameron so unready a European?). Does he assume, perhaps accurately, that all influential Scottish Tories must have been educated in England, or that English history cuckoo-like displaces the past in Scottish schools? (Michael Gove has yet to spread the wings of his angelic death over Scottish education).

Let Mr Cameron be our parable in teaching Dr Brown a lesson. The only people who make foreigners of Scots in England are themselves.

Ireland here as elsewhere is the precedent consistently ducked by Cameron and Co. Long before the Union of 1801 or the Union of 1707, the reductionist Cromwell or the receptionist James VI/I, Culloden or Flodden, the Boyne or Bannockburn, the treaty of Windsor or the treaty of Wedmore, people had been travelling from anywhere to anywhere else in our archipelago, sometimes with horrific effects such as the ruthless raids of Picts and Scots, Angle and Saxons, against the unfortunate inhabitants of the rich plains of what became England. St Patrick, a child of somewhere in Romanised Britain was enslaved in Ireland and led its Christianisation, and the coverts of his converts Christianised Britain and its other islands. Armies might land and predators might grab, with or without a sufficiently hypocritical claim of legality, but still ordinary people, tramps and nomads, single or family, made their way from island to island and made themselves well known where they went. The smaller of the two largest islands was much more easily invaded from England than was the mountainous north of the largest island of all. The results are evident enough today. English and Irish law are akin to one another as neither is to Scots law. The religion of the plurality of the local population is both Ireland and England is episcopalian, whether Protestant or Catholic, where Scotland was far more demotic or congregationalist (with a small 'c'). Of course a great deal of the history of these mobile people remains unwritten and is probably forever lost. In the remotest mountains of Donegal or Argyll the same folktales are told of ancient Celtic lore, the clear result of longago voyagers in currachs or coracles. In certain ways the northern lands on each of the two greater islands built links stronger than they held with the southern parts of their own islands. If Robert Bruce ever saw a spider, it was in Rathlin Island off the coast of Ireland that he saw it. When Bonnie Prince Charlie landed in 1745 in Moidart, it was a Macdonnell of Antrim, landing in Scotland for the first time, who convinced Macdonald of Clanranald that the interests of their vast family network on either side of the North Channel required him to set aside his conviction that an insurrection was impossible, and lead his fellow-Scots to fight for the true king. Spenser knew the south of Ireland with a masterly hold on its topography expressed in his poetry and prose, having grabbed as much of it as he could. Shakespeare spoke of Ireland with an accuracy far superior to his knowledge of Scotland. We have all been mixed up with each other for millennia.

What this means is that Britain down the centuries has been very heavily Hibernicised. Choose your century, and the Irish are invading Britain. Missionaries evangelising, enlightening, and enslaving, mercenaries murdering and managing, migrants for reasons which might become permanent, mythologisers and musicians, and so on and so forth. Of course they supply sufficiently famous representatives to intrude even through the sniffiest snobberies of historians: try the 18th century theatre, and Congreve, Farquahar, Macklin, Goldsmith, Sheridan have every one of them an Irish antecedent. Swift's pamphlet war brought down Marlborough, and Burke's eloquence indicted British administration in America, both in the supreme inescapable ethics and rationality that sharpened their perceptions honed in the smaller island. Call them all rich and rare epiphanies of the blend of our different cultures and you will be right. But none of them had an British–Irish Act of Union to call mother or stepmother.

And what it means is that the English are children of Irish, Welsh, Scots and English, however far back the minglings may go before the various Unions (including that forced on Wales by the half-Welshman Henry VIII). Of course the process accelerated as populations mushroomed. The obviously symbolic result showed itself in recent prime ministers. The Irish to whose invisibility Mr Cameron seems pledged provided progenitors eventuating in James Callaghan, Margaret Thatcher and Tony Blair.

Callaghan's great-grandfather John Garoghan (his grandson changed the name to Callaghan) was born in Ireland of a Union six years old (1806) while Catherine Sullivan, great-grandmother of Margaret Thatcher, was born in Ireland in 1811. Tony Blair's mother was born in Ballyshannon, Co. Donegal in 1923, thus being born outside the UK while still a subject of George V. All this may be very distressing to Mr Cameron in his anxiety to keep the Union of 1707 sacrosanct and unadulterated by subsequent Unions. It is hardly gratifying to the present writer either, given his maternal membership of the Sullivan family however desirably removed from Catherine by many decades, leagues and kindred. James Callaghan's name was unpronounceable by most of his colleagues (Dr Gordon Brown for one always gave it the hard 'g') and its earlier form, the little-known Irish name Garoghan, would have been as difficult. As for the Irish mother from Ballyshannon, Mr Blair proved so successful in avoiding anti-Scottish feeling by eluding as far as possible reference to his Edinburgh birth and to the Edinburgh location of his extremely Anglified school, that his mother's birth was even more disposable until it proved diplomatically desirable.

Mr Cameron's deHibernicisation of history is not entirely deliberate (indeed in his case it is usually doubtful whether to attribute his errors and omissions to contrivance or ignorance). The late 19th century was the summit of frank racism and racialism in public life, and one of its effects was an obsession with racial purity among the elite and its would-be entrants. Whites wanted to avoid the taint of descent from non-white, non-whites if less noisily wanted to avoid that of descent from white. Religion asserted itself with its more outspoken votaries anxious to deny that any ancestors could have been anything other than Protestant (since the Reformation) or Catholic (since St Patrick). This nonsense meant that genealogies were ethnically cleansed. The Irish Catholics held themselves aloof from, and were held in abhorrence by innumerable others who were in fact far from distant cousins. Despite the evidence all around them nobody seemed ready to admit that the Scots might be of Highland or Lowland origin, the Welsh might come from North or South Wales, and that anyone might be Irish with much more variation in movement in and out of Protestantism and Catholicism than any clerics of either faith would want people to know. Poor Mr Cameron has simply inherited this legacy of nasty self-delusion, but the reality is that Union spawned many unions in and out of matrimony including later Unions, and the inhabitants of these islands will continue to mingle whatever constitutional condition pompous persons may term them. If Mr Cameron wants to break his heart, there are much stronger justifications for it, headed by the number of persons in dire poverty throughout the UK that he nominally rules.

The omnipresence of the Irish in Britain brings home another consideration. The Irish have played an outstanding though frequently invisible part in the growth of the labour movement. And well they might. When Parnell addressed a meeting in Boston on 12 January 1880, Wendell Phillips the great anti-slavery orator stood beside him to tell a mass audience that the prosperity in America arose from the produce of western fields coming by water and rail transport to Atlantic ports, and that the profits had been made over Irish bodies. He was speaking of the endless number of diggers, navvies, tarriers, used up and thrown aside in the brutal labour market. Britain's canals and railways were built up from such migrant Irish labour, Catholic or Protestant, frequently rivalling their ethnic and linguistic cousins the Highlanders. The same was true of mining across the North Atlantic, with the Welsh taking the lead there. Now, countless Irish have assimilated one way or another, in the end giving these Micks or Paddies in the family tree no more celebration than Margaret Thatcher gave the Sullivans. But there is no reason for shame, save in the shame of being ashamed. The Irish of all denominations have every reason to be proud of their part in building the labour movement in Britain. And their identity is reaffirmed and celebrated by seeing its presence in an independent Scotland.

Why do the NO-men continue with this absurd comedy that there never was an Irish–British Union? The obvious answer is that while they don't know much history, they can see the minefield in the potato patch. The height of Irish migration to Britain was during the great famine of 1845–52. It had been high, ever since the Union of 1800, and it remained high to the end of the century: and it was migration, not immigration, for they were all in the one country, the British–Irish UK. But the huge influx of Irish, with a much higher proportion of Catholic and Gaelic-speakers (some monoglot and many near-monoglot), many more from the quick, resourceful, habitually poverty-stricken mountain men, distinguished the famine from previous and subsequent migrations. Worse still, they brought cholera and various other diseases made epidemic by famine. Myths circulated much more in the USA than in Britain and the Empire but widely enough there that the British government intended to wipe out the Irish. This was nonsense: but it was assisted by the asinine utterances of brilliant economists unable to separate paper theory from practical events, and also by doctrinaire administrators terrified of impairing economic rules by excessive relief or public works. The real effect was that, much more than in the 1707 Union, the Union of 1801 had proclaimed its confidence in its superiority for governing Ireland over the nominally separate and actually subordinate Irish Parliament 1782–1800. And the Famine left the great success of the UK horribly failed almost at the heart of Empire. It reverberates to this day. Mr Cameron and the NO-men cannot admit their beloved Union of 1707 included a much-denounced Union of 1801. The NO-men foolishly preach an obviously bogus claim of perpetual successes for their Union, but it sinks from foolish little fraud to flat failure once the other Union is included and surveyed from 1845 to 1852. You can hardly claim your Union was the best in human history when you have a deficit of one million five hundred souls dead over a decade with the same number or more having fled from their island home only to die on board ship or at their port of destination in Britain or elsewhere.

All of this 'best in the world' rubbish is in any case demeaning to its users and hearers, and it is a measure of their contempt for us all, Scots or English or Welsh or Irish, that Messrs Cameron and Co. revert to it. Can they really think we are stupid enough to be convinced or even impressed by it? Can they not realise that people who may sympathise in some degree with NO-voting may feel they cannot with any self-respect support the cause preached with such stupid cynicism? No country is the best in the world, and no other one is, either.

To make matters worse, and deepen the uncertainly as to whether the stupidity or cynicism is the prevailing wind among the NO-spokesmen, surely they realise that a large number of Scottish voters are descended from Famine migrants and know exactly how to evaluate claims of the Union as the best in the world. The Irish and the Scots are both historically conscious people, and not in the gung-ho spirit dear to *Our Island Story* and Mr Michael Gove. Losers linger on their loss. Even if they didn't, the most vociferous supporters of the Union in recent years have been supporters of the Glasgow Rangers football team. It's worth our remembering that it didn't begin that way, when late in the 19th century clergymen of Protestant and Catholic persuasions took similar steps to keep their youthful charges off the street corners by organising football clubs which were then despised by gentlemen's football clubs. Mutual hostilities arose in the 1920s when the bitter memories of the Irish insurrection of 1916 were in retrospect seen as treachery by soldiers' families and as victimisation by sympathisers with those shot (although frequently not with their rebellion), and stories circulated about Catholics taking jobs left by Protestants serving in the war. Even then the rival chants were mostly stupid and the songs anachronistic more than anything else. Glasgow Celtic songs were chiefly Irish, romanticising a method of warfare Michael Collins and his associates would have regarded as suicidally imitative of the more incompetent engagements of World War I, while Orange songs were often either unintentionally camp or intentionally satirical. But in recent years nastier exchanges developed, as the 30 years war in Northern Ireland waxed and waned. One particularly ugly composition (sounding more like a decomposition) was sung by Rangers football crowds requesting the Celtic supporters to return to Ireland while jeering at them as refugees from the Famine. The thing was as ludicrous as it was libellous: it denounced the Irish for receiving welfare state support while supposedly aiding the Germans by lighting the Atlantic and Channel ports during World War II. But it was violently resented by Catholics (and possibly by descendants of the many Irish Protestants who also fled from the Famine) and it served to keep the Famine alive as an alienating memory. Neither the Rangers mob, nor the Prime Ministerial paeans of praise for the Union under which the Famine happened, are likely to increase the NO vote. Above all, the obvious fact that the Prime Minister has no inkling of the hideous memories his foolish fine fantasy furnishes adds insult to the injuries. And he only wanted to be nice.

Ireland may be blotted out of the vision of the Union peddled by Mr

David Cameron, because it calls his Union hymns into some question, but it also has its relevance to remind us of things best avoided. The NO crowd frequently abuse nationalism, with what they take to be apposite analogies from the recent history of Bosnia or the less recent history of Germany. At the same time they produce stirring nationalism in support of the Union. They either deny their own nationalism or else pretend to deny it. All that 'best in the world' stuff is nationalism at its worst. But their nationalism also keeps coming back to the strength-though-joy they preach to justify endless expense on political violence, whether weapons of mass destruction or ships so much bigger than those that caused World War I through German–British naval rivalry. Scottish nationalism, whether SNP, or Green Party, or preached by Margo MacDonald, abominates violence, repudiates the idea of a nation trying to prove itself by weapon-flashing, and firmly rejects at all times the bloodshed to which Irish nationalism in the 20th century so foolishly succumbed. Ireland fell prey to the madness perpetrated by the international holocaust embracing the world in 1914–18, and in protest against that war became a pawn among the belligerents and a clone of what it thought it was opposing. Scotland wanted no part of that, and was in fact true to the non-violent tradition which so many Scots followed in admiration for such Irish leaders as Daniel O'Connell and Michael Davitt. The IRA simply painted British imperialism green and went on from there, wallowing in its killing potential with all of the fervour of the British Sea Lords and Air Marshals. The UVF and such Protestant militaristic bodies synthesised IRA methods with its parent British nationalism in the raw, flavoured with Glasgow Rangers and Ulster Unionist delicacies.

The eradication of Ireland and its Union from Mr Cameron's discourse sacrifices the entire island, not simply what is now the Republic. Mr Cameron is fond of saluting the Olympic achievement of Team GB'. But 'Team GB' excluded Northern Ireland by definition. Northern Ireland athletes who wanted to compete had to seek status under the Republic, after all the preceding years of Whitehall and Westminster promise of support for all in Northern Ireland who wanted to remain part of the UK. It would have been so easy to rally to 'Team UK'. The long-sought peace in Northern Ireland depends on building the institutions of peace including identity in place of shadows of GB or of the Republic. What Northern Ireland wanted was to be real and to be treated as such, instead of merely being fodder for the rhetoric of whatever Dublin or London politicians chose to exploit their situation. All of David Cameron's wallowing in self-congratulation from the Olympics, and attempts to use them against the democratically elected government of Scotland, drain away. Just as he discarded UK for GB in Northern Ireland, he would junk Britain for England whenever electoral advantage beckoned. It is in fact all he has been trained to do, and the immediate necessity of bribing, bullying and blackmailing the Scots has jerked Toryism out of the even tenor of its English way. Whether Scotland leaves or remains in the UK, Britain will revert to its historic Englishness.

But Labour, the traditional party of Scots and Irish whether in Scotland or Wales or England, must surely differ from this boiling down of identities? Surely it would not butcher Northern Ireland to make a London holiday? Dr Gordon Brown's quest for Britishness whether he is in or out of government resulted in his introducing a volume edited by Matthew d'Ancona, *Being British: The Search for the Values that Bind the Nation*. The wide net catching so many contributors resulted in works of varying value. The then Roman Catholic Archbishop of Westminster, His Eminence Cormac Cardinal Murphy-O'Connor, began by correctly noting Professor Linda Colley's famous treatise *Britons* according to which, he noted:

> The concept of Britishness in the eighteenth century was invented by a Protestant nation in order to unify these islands, promote trade, consolidate the monarchy, foster an empire, and make the country strong enough to resist Catholic Europe.

The ease with which the word 'nation' is attached to Britain and Britishness by officials or prominent public persons apparently gives no difficulty to those who would complain should we speak of British nationalism – but let us follow His Eminence further:

> It is with a heavy heart that a catholic like myself can only agree when someone says that what we describe as Britishness can be traced back to the civil war and the Acts of Union. Indeed so, and the presence of Catholics in this historically Protestant state was for a long time prob-

lematic, particularly and most severely in the north of Ireland, where Catholics suffered a discrimination that should have been removed before bitterness erupted so murderously there. Catholics in these islands know only too well that this country has promoted a version of Britishness that denied them liberty of religion and human rights simply because they held that the authority of the Pope is central to the church founded by Christ. Within the recent past, for example, many Irish people coming to Britain read signs outside factories and houses that said 'No Irish Need Apply'. As a British citizen born of Irish parents, these issues have been very close to me.

Passing over the inevitable thought from a Catholic like myself 'Did anyone ever call him Spud-O'Connor?' his take on Britain and Britishness is all too accurate however self-interested it may appear. The speed with which defenders of the union choose 'tolerance' as its defining feature tastes sour if you derive from the wrong end of it. 'Liberty' was synonymous with anti-Catholicism in these islands including those with Catholic majorities. William of Orange saw Liberty as equal rights for all, such as his fellow Dutch of all Christian denominations practised: his supporters in Britain and Ireland did not.

This may hint at the desire of David Cameron to keep Ireland quarantined if not actually frozen, but what of Gordon Brown? Labour has consistently been the party protecting Catholic education and opposing discrimination. Yet the eminent historian Paul Bew, now my Lord Bew and vigorous in defence of the Union, told readers of *Being British* (p.256):

> The prime minister, Gordon Brown, in an article entitled 'We Must Defend the Union' in the *Daily Telegraph* of 25 March 2008, opened with a loud call to arms to the British people, warning that the benefits conferred by the Union were in danger of being lost unless the British people defended it against secessionist forces. But it turned out that in the rest of the article, the Union that was to be defended was only a mainland phenomenon – English, Scottish, and Welsh, but decidedly not Irish. it was the mutually beneficial economic, cultural and political interactions of the larger island that were hailed as positive – no contribution apparently could be listed on behalf of the Northern Irish... in the short term, this new definition of Britishness was politically maladroit – it is, after all, supposed to be one great selling point of the Good Friday Agreement to the Unionist community that it

guarantees on the basis of consent their position within the United Kingdom.

In other words the Union being defended is not the one so many British and Irish have died for in Ulster. And what has a Labour prime minister to do with a newspaper saturated with galloping reaction such as the *Daily Telegraph*? If the Union demands betrayals like that, and allies like this, the sooner Labour defends its beliefs and traditions where they are safest, the better. And they are safest in an independent Scotland where weapons of mass destruction cannot usurp the funds that should go to welfare, education and health, and where Socialism will not be sacrificed to the alliance with the *Daily Telegraph*.

Unionists talk as if an independent Scotland will cut off its links with England and Wales. On the contrary an independent Scotland looks forward to real relations as fellow sovereign states with the Republic of Ireland and the UK, and building up further links with all parts of the UK including Wales and Northern Ireland. We will want to celebrate the part played by the Irish whether Protestant or Catholic in the building of modern Scotland including honour to such Irish-Scottish makers of Scottish Socialist ideology as James Connolly, John Wheatley, and the navvy poet Patrick MacGill whose *Children of the Dead End* and *The Rat Pit* gave his personal witness to the foul conditions of migrant labour, male and female, in early 20th century Scotland. The Scotland we want to build must never lose sight of the horrors through which our ancestors struggled, whether Irish or not. We have to eradicate poverty and to know it we must study the sufferings of Irish, Welsh, English, Italians, Poles, Jews, Muslims, Slavs and every kind of contributor to our past including the native Scots – Highland, Lowland, urban, Border, island or mainland. We will use that inheritance to save other countries and societies from such poverty as infected Scotland. We will dishonour our past if we surrender to the great political parties with their obsessive devotion to war and its vampire demands for endless money. Labour under its present leaders is as ready to waste the wealth of the UK on Trident as are the Tories and Liberal Democrats. And the record of Ireland as a state is a good example for an independent Scotland, in its consistent policy of working for peace instead of merely using it as a camouflage for war.

For the better happiness and productivity of everyone, whether Scotland becomes independent or not, it is obviously best to inform ourselves of what knowledge is available to us, instead of competing in silly fortune-telling about the future. Since what is at stake is the effect of one country in our archipelago changing status to independence, nothing could be more sensible than to look at the previous country to make that change. We would have to make allowance for the tragedy of violence in the Irish story, with thankfulness that the Scots won't touch violence in seeking independence. And one of the first things to notice is that for over half a century after independence the pound sterling was linked in Ireland and the then remaining UK. For most of that time every Irish pound note carried the statement that it was worth one pound sterling in London. Then why did George Osborne, Ed Balls and Danny Alexander strut stuff at Scotland to say that never would Scotland have such a link with the rest of the UK after independence, carefully concealing the truth about the pound's history of currency union with Ireland, indeed saying such a thought was impossible. They either lied together or were ignorant together, and on either ground they proved themselves unfit to rule the financial roost in the UK whether or not it contains Scotland. In either event they show that the Unionist case is so weak that it has to conceal and deny the historical truth.

The vote on independence on 18 September 2014 is a vote about the future, but despite all the propaganda from the Unionists, we do not and cannot know what the future really holds. If enough of the Unionists' weapons of mass destruction should blow us all up on 19 September 2014 there would be no future for us. So our decisions must be taken in the light of the past, and of the treatment of that past by defenders of that past. And if the Unionists can only make their case by pretending Ireland never existed, that it never was in the UK or that no part of it still is, the Unionists are at war with both geography and history. We follow them at our peril. And in spite of all they say, and don't say, Ireland forms part of these islands, and Northern Ireland remains in the United Kingdom.

YES, David Cameron, YES, YES, YES, there really is an elephant in the room.

CHAPTER SEVEN

Thank you, Edwin Morgan, Thank you, J.K. Rowling

OWEN DUDLEY EDWARDS

...I strongly advise you not to use the words England and English when you mean what is larger than England and English...

Let me illustrate this by one further remark. There are two conceptions which are of great importance to students of international law; the one nationality, the other domicile. Now there is no such thing as English nationality, and there is no such thing as British domicile. The Englishman, the Scot, the Irishman, the Canadian, the Australian – all of these have a nationality in common; ...But there is no such thing as British domicile – because there is no one system common to all the British dominions...

Frederic William Maitland (1850–1906), c.1888
Constitutional History of England – a Course of Lectures

At seventy I thought I had come through, like parting a bead curtain in Port Said, to something that was shadowy before, figures and voices of late times that might be surprising you. The beads clash faintly behind me as I go forward. No candle-light please, keep that for Europe. Switch the whole thing right on. When I go in I want it bright, I want to catch whatever is there in full sight.

Edwin Morgan (1920–2010) 'Epilogue: *Seven Decades*' (1990)

EDWIN MORGAN WAS a great poet in a great generation of Scottish poets such as Hugh MacDiarmid, Norman MacCaig, Sorley Maclean, Sydney Goodsir Smith, Iain Crichton Smith, George Mackay Brown, most of whom wanted Independence for Scotland. He was also a great translator bringing poetry from across the globe into our speech of these islands. And he was gay, sublimely affirming the right of love between man and man, woman and woman, woman and man. He made our world a richer, more beautiful and more honest one. He died, leaving a great legacy to the cause of Scottish Independence. He also left it a million pounds.

J.K. Rowling is a great writer for children and now for adults as well. Thanks to her fascinating series of novels about Harry Potter, she has stemmed the tide drawing children away from reading and helped millions to recover its joy. She has used her wealth to fight agonising and destructive disease, and she has used her literary gifts to fight racism, witch-hunting, snobbery, child victimisation, literary fraud and journalistic lies. She is a friend of Dr Gordon Brown and has been proud to be so when he was under endless belittlement by scurrilous newspaper attacks. She has now contributed a million pounds against the cause of Scottish Independence.

Scotland has every reason to be proud of both, and to make the survivor forever welcome here.

The despicable attacks on Twitter & co. against J.K. Rowling must be scorned by every believer in Scottish Independence. Her right to make what she thinks is the best use of her money in the Referendum fight is one no Scot can deny if independence means anything. It is not independence but slavery to the worst and most degrading bullying to make such attacks. It lowers those who make it to the level of the newspaper moguls, many of whom have no real country at all and have been dictating their journalists' biases through the whole Referendum campaign, to deny us a country.

We do not know if any of these vicious attacks on J.K. Rowling were actually by supporters of Scottish Independence. None of them may be. It would be only one more dirty trick of the kind so many newspaper owners have authorised, to try to arouse hatred against Independence supporters. It is easily possible also that it is the work of minor Unionist politicians. We know Dr Gordon Brown would not touch such action, and nothing Mr David Cameron or Mr Nick Clegg have done seems consistent with it. But their gallantry does not exist in all ranks. We can think of many Unionist politicians who would have such attacks made on J.K. Rowling to blacken the name of the YES campaign. And you can probably think of quite a few yourself. It might remind you of Nigel Farage calling the Scots racists when they protested against his campaign against immigrants. J.K. Rowling would not be in the least surprised if Unionist press or politicians were proved to have been behind all these attacks on her. Harry Potter is victimised by such a character and the endless lies it produces to blacken the names of innocent folk: the excruciatingly horrible journalist Rita Skeeter who carries out her character assassinations while pretending the utmost friendship for the person she is trying to destroy. You would have to range through the whole of English literature to find so accurate a satire on that kind of witch-hunting manipulator.

J.K. Rowling is no enemy to Scotland. She deserves our pride and our gratitude. We wish she was on our side, but she has done so much for humanity that we must always know her as our true friend. We have all been Harry Potter under her enchantment.

We have other friends of humanity who have lined up against us. Of course many people claimed by the NO-men have certainly not come out for 'NO'. Pope Francis has made it clear that Independence for Scotland needs to be approached with the greatest care. He calls for the need to use tweezers, that is to say instruments to keep the questions as accurately and judiciously handled as possible. That does not mean pompous ignoramuses telling us they will doom us if we say YES. The Pope would want a humane system, a compassionate society, a rejection of false values of materialism. He is naturally all in favour of our denying a harbour to Trident. He would abominate the *Daily Mail* pretending that he says YES voters will commit mortal sin.

Catholics voting YES will do so in the belief that we can serve God better in a small independent country than in a power-drunk ex-giant trying to pretend to itself and everyone else that the sun never sets on it. We want a country in which people are proud to be what we are. We want to be part of the world instead of running away from it. Our children mature by studying books that tell of human struggles against oppression everywhere, great books like Harper Lee's *To Kill a Mockingbird,* which is now being taken off the school syllabus in England because it isn't English enough. It is a beautiful, honest, sensitive, inspirational work telling us of the cruelty and degradation which African Americans suffered, and how some American whites worked to help them find freedom. NO says No to *To Kill a Mockingbird*.

And President Barack Obama really and truly publicly supports NO. Now, unlike J.K. Rowling he isn't a citizen of Scotland, he doesn't live here though he would be very welcome. But many of us made no secret of our hoping the USA would end its institutional and populist racism, and some of us were able to go there and work to help the African Americans in their struggle where they gave wonderful examples of non-violent action.

President Obama is perfectly entitled to express his views on whether Scotland should be independent or not. If we can tell him he ought to close down the horror camp at Guantanamo where in the name of the rule of law, the USA with the aid of the UK kidnaps people, imprisons them, tortures them, and refuses to try them – if we say 'pluck out the Guantanamo in thine own eye, Barack', we admit that he can express his views even if his prisoners can't express theirs. He may think that he is being a friend to the UK but it is a rather condescending friendship. Poor David Cameron says he wants the Scots to decide, and then runs round the world beseeching EU Presidents about to quit office, Spanish ministers in economic collapse, Presidents and Presidential candidates of the USA, to tell the Scots to vote NO. It isn't actually very good psychological warfare to posture as a great power, to try to bribe the Scots to stay in the UK as if it is a great Power, and to ask the world and his wife to tell the Scots what to do since the UK is apparently too weak or too ignorant to sell its own case, or else that its case is so bad that it has to pump itself up by getting testimonials from anyone who might trade NO-saying in some God-forsaken political bargain. Of course President Obama is above that kind of political trading. But he is imprisoned by what President Eisenhower so rightly warned us all against, the military industrial complex, which wants us to keep Trident. To please the USA, keep the UK a warfare state. Too bad about welfare. President Obama has even censured his wretched allies for cutting their Defence budgets, matteradam what happens to their health and their poor.

It is one world, so let President Obama tell us what he thinks we ought to do. The problem about his telling us, is not that he isn't part of us, but that he is. If President Obama were a reactionary oaf in hot competition for the title of the worst President of the United States, as his predecessor was, it would matter far less than it does. President Bush knew what he owned, including the Prime Minister of the UK ('yo-Blair'), and he knew how to call it to heel without the approval of the UK population, never mind Scotland. He knew how to patronise Dr Gordon Brown by assuring the world Dr Brown wasn't a dour Scot – he left it open as to whether he meant that Dr Brown wasn't dour, or that he wasn't a Scot, but he knew Scots were dour so it was polite to say they weren't when you know they were. (He was, after all, trained in race relations in Texas.)

But Barack Obama is one of the most intelligent men who has ever been President of the USA. He is the author of a literary masterpiece. His campaign for the Presidency won the heart of the decent world. He won partly in protest against the agony of slavery, the cruelty of segregation, the brutality of the Klu Klux Klan, the horror of unequal justice under law, the decades of ruling-class equivocation, deceit, denial, destruction. He showed himself the justifiable heir to those victims, the proof of the righteousness of the cause of racial justice. He won a constituency which the pollsters were too self-satisfied and too snobbish to realise existed and would vote, or if they did realise it, they lacked the language to talk to it, be trusted by it, or comprehend it.

And President Obama brought back dignity to the US Presidency, gave art to Presidential oratory such as it had lacked since Franklin Roosevelt, restored wit to the heights of Kennedy, and social wisdom to the domestic leadership once given by Lyndon Johnson. That Republican gerrrymandering lost Obama the House, and intransigence frustrated his attempts at political negotiation, were less his fault than his misfortune. But that very rejoicing in his victory and confidence in his integrity made him ours in ways no previous President could claim. A well-meaning if mistaken intervention from the President of the United States merited no greater reaction than mild wonder that David Cameron or Douglas Alexander should so painfully exhibit their admission that they could not defend the UK on their own, whether because they were inadequate, or their case was inadequate. But that Barack Obama should join the NO-men hurt. His motives were painfully obvious, and were purely based on the selfish interests of two nuclear powers (or perhaps in the case of the UK, half-power). His place in our hearts came from different logic. And in a response in which Alex Salmond showed his own dignity and affection, it was all summed up with the answer 'YES we can!'. That as to answer the Obama of big power bloody-mindedness by the Obama who had won our hearts. And the new Obama is no match for the old. He gave us the slogan to take us to victory, the self-respect to endure for it, and the laughter and love with which to face the miserable pessimism of the big guns. They may make what they choose of the Obama among the 'haves': we take our proud place with the Obama of the 'have-nots'.

And 'YES we can!' has another moral to point. In history when a great man turned his back on his radical past, angry former admirers would repudiate him: 'Just for a handful of silver he left us' cried Robert Browning of William Wordsworth in his 'The Lost Leader'. That does not, and cannot, apply in the struggle for an independent Scotland. We want an independent Scotland to welcome the NO-men whom we once admired, and help us to admire them again, to give Gordon Brown the admiration he deserves but which Westminster never gave him, and Whitehall only pretended.

Ironically despite the exaggerated hostilities of the Democratic Party primary campaign in 2008, and appropriately for their subsequent collaboration, Hillary Clinton is in the exact situation of Barack Obama, as regards Scotland. She like he opts for NO on an obvious narrow interpretation of American self-interest. And her doing so does not devalue one iota her great crusade to bring American women and the women of the world to the level of equality which is so rightly theirs. In Hillary Clinton's case Scotland on its side still has support to give in a continuing struggle, not simply in refusing to dishonour former affection. Let us hope as human beings that she will contest the Presidency and that this time she will win. And if Scotland votes YES then she may learn a lesson which could be of great value to her in the Presidency. It is that her claims on our world-wide support have nothing to do with big bombs in or out of our harbours where they trespass against the wishes of the inhabitants. And if YES we can, so also YES she can!

The great historian of law F.W. Maitland, lecturing to his Cambridge students in 1888, denied the existence of English nationality. That was true of 1888, and it tells us much of the vagaries of our sense of identity. Time frays his definition, but it is worth remembering, apart from its lucidity. It helps explain the curious anger some English express, not very articulately, when Scottish independence is treated as possible. To Maitland in 1888, English, Scot, Irish, Canadian, Australian were traitors should they 'side with' the UK's enemies in wartime. A hundred and twenty-five years later, Australia, Canada and Ireland would not necessarily be bound by the UK's being at war, and today Scots and English can have no common constitutional confidence at least until 18 September is past. But the firm deposit of belief thus enshrined in Maitland's posthumously published, widely used lecture text *Constitutional History of England* expressed the conventional wisdom of the British-Irish establishment, and children in Scotland, Ireland, Wales no less than children in England were taught at school to learn by heart in their infancy: the lines by Ann (1782–1866) and Jane (1783–1824) Taylor's *Hymns for Infant Minds*, 1. 'A Child's Hymn of Praise'.

> I thank the goodness and the grace
> Which on my birth have smiled,
> And made me, in these Christian days,
> A happy English child.

Nancy Mitford in the 1950s would point out that it showed one was 'U' or upper-class to say 'England' rather than 'Britain' and even historians as great and as left-wing as A.J.P. Taylor (1906–90) would conform to that: his *English History 1914–1945* (1965) is probably the greatest book ever written on British history in the 20th century, and it would be silly to feel aggrieved when a book is as good as that. Yet its titular conventionality is our scientific indication of the social effects of Maitland's doctrine and the other Taylors' rhyme so ruthlessly required of children between the Napoleonic and Second World Wars. Maitland would doubtless have deplored the distortion of his deliberations.

Yet the distinction of England, Ireland, Scotland and Wales runs very deep through our islands, and when we look at a grip as longlasting on our minds as Shakespeare's, it could hardly be clearer. The eve of battle at Harfleur as imagined in *Henry V* pointedly flourishes representative soldiers from Wales, Scotland and Ireland. Shakespeare could feed what we might call the proto-Mitford germ by making the dying John of Gaunt in *Richard II* hymn:

> ... this sceptr'd isle, ...
> This precious stone set in the silver sea,
> Which serves it in the office of a wall,
> Or as a moat defensive to a house,
> Against the envy of less happier lands;
> This blessed plot, this realm, this England

the beauty of whose rendition by, say, John Gielgud, obliterates its absurdities of chauvinism although when it was written the isle was two separate kingdoms with separate kings. But before Harfleur a different chauvinism is required whence the different lands of the islands speak regardless of whether and how much Henry V was their actual ruler. And it is not quite the fix to ensure England's predominance later generations may think. The English may predominate but, one way or another, the Welsh always win (Shakespeare was partly Welsh and *Henry V Part 1* originally included lines in Welsh, and *King Lear* and *Cymbeline* have Welsh origins and so did the Tudors). But the Scot on the English throne required something more than multinational tableaux: *Macbeth* was the necessary prescription to entertain and educate. The story itself was part of James's genealogical family legend, and Shakespeare may not even have known that the real Macbeth was a good king, who killed his younger rival Duncan in a fair fight if he killed him at all (Macbeth's more serious danger lasting well beyond Duncan was Duncan's father the Abbot Crinan). Shakespeare may have believed Macbeth a tyrant and regicide but he did invent the worst part of Duncan's murder, his being a guest in Macbeth's house, under his protection and in his trust. There may be a hint of this being generically Scottish, but no more: James was after all Shakespeare's company's patron.

On the other hand James would have no objection to a message that the Scots were barbaric, or at least more so than the English, and that the English must help their lawful king to civilise them. The process culminates in the irrelevant and dotty conclusion when King Malcolm turns all the Scottish thanes into Earls how English: both titles in fact derive from

Norse words. There may have been a covert message visible to James and to Shakespeare, but not widely elsewhere: Macbeth murders Duncan but Duncan's son succeeds Macbeth – Elizabeth murdered Mary, but Mary's son succeeded Elizabeth. But the message of England's superior civilisation was to the forefront of the play in the later Acts, above all the English doctor's testimony to the healing powers of the English king, Edward the Confessor. That could also be turned into a personal compliment for James who liked to think of his own powers in that respect, as well as his divine appointment easily ascribable to the Saxon saint-king. So might the use of witches in the play, given James's literary and theological activities in their detection. But the cumulative effect would certainly have been to tell the Globe's English audience what a barbarous fratricidal superstitious lot they were now tied to, regardless of the fact that recent English history had been far more fratricidal (as impressively recorded in Shakespeare's lays of the Wars of the Roses). Macbeth has in fact become the supreme magnet of superstition in the performance of Shakespeare plays, the title itself being too perilous to be spoken (rather like J.K. Rowling's demonic Lord Voldemort's name), so that it gets called 'The Scottish Play' (which it certainly is not). It is also one of the most wonderful plays in the English language borne on sublime poetry.

But we know very little about Shakespeare's actual views on major questions (a Welsh bias eased into the plays is minor). The usual 'as Shakespeare says' means that Shakespeare thought it appropriate for some character with whose convictions he may have shared nothing. We should remember the film mogul Sam Goldwyn looking at the large funeral crowd for his former (very much former) colleague Louis B. Mayer; 'Give the public what they want –!' This doesn't mean Shakespeare of the Scottish Enlightenment betray their principles or their countries by a touch of reason to sweeten their real intent: For Shakespeare surely the preservation and strengthening of theatre, for the Scottish Enlightenment to educate the English majority looming over them. So the great Scots writers took the lead in inventing England wrapped up in philosophy honed in Scotland, purged their writings of Scotticisms so as not to lose the English market, flung in the occasional sugar in the shape of a graceful but ultimately trivial compliment to the English. That the English were the strongest of the four countries was ultimately less important than that they were the most numerous and hence the public needing small payments to make them pay big and be taught in the process. The Scottish Enlightenment was very much a product of its universities with their belief in education for the greatest possible number, later called 'the democratic intellect', unlike the English Oxford and Cambridge functioning chiefly as finishing schools for a wealthy elite or European obscurantist servants of an established ruling church and state. Whether for financial, political, military or administrative glory, the Union was there to further Scottish influence and, however covertly, Scots authority. When it couldn't be disguised, as when George III made his Scots tutor, the Earl of Brute, Prime Minister in 1762, the English writhed at their subjection. Macaulay's second essay on the elder Pitt tells the story:

> The cry of all south was that the public offices, the army, the navy, were filled with high-cheeked Drummonds and Erskines, Macdonalds and Macgillivrays, who could not talk a Christian tongue, and some of whom had but lately begun to wear Christian breeches. All the old jokes on hills without trees, girls without stockings, men eating the food of horses, pails emptied from the fourteenth story, were pointed against these lucky adventurers. To the honour of the Scots it must be said, that their prudence and their pride restrained them from retaliation. Like the princess in the Arabian tale, they stopped their ears tight, and, unmoved by the shrillest notes of abuse, walked on, without once looking round, straight towards the Golden Fountain.

Dr Gordon Brown, fond of the word 'prudence' when he first became chancellor of the Exchequer, had a somewhat similar situation 234 years later, and in his case the Golden Fountain was modernised under the word 'Britain'. Certainly no Scot since Bute preserved so unwavering a devotion to 'Britain' in the face of so many ugly lies and so many repetitive jests. Fleet Street humour through Punch and into Private Eye consists largely of telling endless variations on the same jokes.

But the Scots found themselves having to teach the English how to make anti-Scottish jokes, or at least what looked like them. David Hume (1711–76) wrote 'Of National Character' in the 1740s:

> We may often remark a wonderful mixture of manners and characters in the same nation, speaking the same language, and subject to the same government. And in this particular the ENGLISH are the most remarkable of any people that perhaps ever were in the world. Nor is this to be ascribed to the mutability and uncertainty of their climate, or to any other physical causes; since all these causes take place in the neighbouring country of SCOTLAND, without having the same effect. ... the ENGLISH government is a mixture of monarchy, aristocracy, and democracy. The people in authority are composed of gentry and merchants. All sects of religion are to be found among them. And the great liberty and independency, which every man enjoys, allows him to display the manners peculiar to him. Hence the ENGLISH, of any people in the universe, have the least of a national character, unless this very singularity may pass for such.

The giveaway word here is of course 'universe'. The Enlightened Scots were far too scientific to generalise especially to the uttermost limits of absurdity. It is a misfortune to humanity that so few modern historians will credit the great minds of times past with senses of humour. Hume was talking delicious nonsense, and was far too intelligent not to know it. But in any case whether formally writing history or otherwise, his system was that of the clever unscrupulous schoolboy who looked up the answers at the back of the book before studying the algebraic problem, and who grew up to write history which should illustrate the conclusions on which he chose to decide. He must have chuckled grimly over the supposed omnipresence of all sects in England when Catholicism and non-conformists of all kinds were restrained by penal legislation. National characteristics themselves are one of the most widespread human delusions, being used so frequently to pejorative effect (see Macaulay on English creations of Scots). But to acquit the most frequent lampooners using allegations of supposed national character, as revelatory of their own national character, was to mix flattery and satire to delicious bibulous effects. As J.H. Goring (probably a Scot) wrote in 1909:

> The Germans live in Germany,
> The Romans live in Rome,
> The Turkeys live in Turkey,
> But the English live at home.

Be he Scot or Scots-descended, Goring was a crude version of the Scots invention of England throughout the Union. At an early stage they decided that England was much too important to be left to the English whether in local profit, imperial plunder, or ideological propaganda. Essentially Hume started it with his *History of England* which began as *History of Great Britain* and worked its way backwards in time (as we were saying apropos the answers at the back of the book). Professor Christopher Harvie, perhaps the leading historian of Scottish nationalism in politics and culture, drew up a list of Scottish inventors of England to which many of us enjoy adding: Smollett, Hume, Boswell, Scott, Byron, Hugh Miller, Carlyle, Macaulay, Gladstone, Ruskin, Stevenson, Conan Doyle, J.M. Barrie, John Buchan, A.G. Macdonnell, Eric Linklater, J.K. Rowling. What could be more English than Dr Johnson, Ivanhoe, Oliver Cromwell, Long John Silver, Sherlock Holmes and Dr Watson, Peter Pan, Harry Potter? But they have been immortally shaped for us by Scots. Granted that some of these authors were born in England: as Byron put it in 'I was born half a Scot and raised a whole one and others also were half-Scots whose half was not wee'. Granted that some of them also tried reinventing Scotland: How far did they invent Britain?

The answer is that most of them did. And if England was so frequently a Scottish literary conceit, Britain was certainly intended to assert the title-deeds held in partnership. Dr Gordon Brown's recent book-title *My Scotland, Our Britain* is undeniable if unnecessary: of course Scotland is also part of our Britain as it is part of our Archipelago, Our Europe, Our Atlantic, Our World, Our Solar System, and Our Universe. To make the point he wants to make, his title should read *My Scotland, Our United Kingdom*, but although his book makes gallant attempts to imply that text in its sermons, it seems awkward and insufficiently cuddly to get into the big print. It was all so much easier in the 18th century until the French and then the Irish got at it. The Scotsman James Thomson (1700–48) put it into song:

> When Britain first, at heaven's command,
> Arose from out the azure main,
> Arose, arose, arose from out the azure main,
> This was the charter, the charter of the land,
> And guardian angels sung this strain:

> Rule, Britannia! Britannia, rule the waves!
> Britons never will be slaves.

It was performed triumphantly in Alfred, a Masque (1740) with music by Thomas Augustine Arne (1710–78), suitably improved by both creators in ensuing years. It was interestingly blasphemous since angels at a birth were traditionally associated with the birth of Jesus Christ, but Elizabeth had previously turned that trick by supplanting the Virgin Mary in Christian devotion with her own popular title 'the Virgin Queen', and James VI having become James I justified his visible caresses for the Duke of Buckingham with 'Christ had his John and I have my George'. Religion was expected to do its bit for the King. But which King? Alfred was supposedly a tribute for the anniversary of accession to the Hanoverian George I (reigned 1714–27) whose Queen never saw England having been imprisoned by her husband for life for alleged adultery (irrespective of his own); it was implied it honoured his son who hated him, George II (reigned 1727–60); it was patronised by George II's son Frederick (who hated but predeceased his father). King Alfred of England (849–901) was one of the greatest kings who ever lived anywhere, militarily, culturally, constitutionally, but it created an ominous precedent for the deification of Britain apart from the prostitution of his name to aggrandise these Hanoverians. Britain had had legal existence only since 1707 and was now identified with a king, however good, whose land was England. When the '45 began something more terrestrial while still theological was required, whence 'God Save the King' adopted during the insurrection.

Britain would continue to be a Scottish creation however successful as a British/Irish cult, at least among Hanoverian supporters. Left to themselves the English seem to have thought of themselves as English and their country, however insular its present frontiers, as England. Scott worked endlessly keeping up with the idea of Britain for the future, with England and Scotland separately celebrated in their past. Simultaneously and far more successfully he made his fellow-Lowlanders acknowledge and admire a kinship with the previously abominated Highlanders, by the ruthless expedient of selling Highland dress metaphorically if not literally to George IV, (duly paraded in tartan trews in 1822) and, more attractively, his poem 'The Lady of the Lake' and his novel *Rob Roy* made the

Highlands win the hearts of the rest of the archipelago. Yet neither prettified what they were vindicating beyond Scott's achievement in landscape artistry. But Scott left his Scotland to Scottish posterity as their united country, whereas his Britain however extolled would always be two fatherlands fascinating in their differences. The next generation acquiesced in the English hold on British identity. Carlyle maintained his Scottishness with his accent and it must be added, with his curiosity of oratorical and literary style: but he used 'England' for 'Britain' however ludicrous his personal identification with Englishness. Macaulay, a Londoner with a Cockney voice, maintained his magic narrative of intrigue and warfare in Scotland and Ireland under the umbrella of History of England: Hume had been more titularly honest however questionable his conclusions. Stevenson and Conan Doyle would play the same trick of recreating an Edinburgh which they called London, and Scott had already done it in time with Ivanhoe's unreconstructed Saxons being drawn on latter-day Jacobite models, the Normans owing something to Whig profiteers. Britain could be kept going by Scots through games of time and space, no doubt ultimately inspiring Dr Who. J.M. Barrie may have played the cleverest Britannification of them all, with Hebridean in Mary Rose stealing a London girl whose son returns from World War One to find her a ghost, and in Peter_Pan his own dead Scottish brother Londonised to become uncrowned king of a deCelted land of perpetual youth. J.K. Rowling brilliantly reversed Dr Johnson's morose description of the road to London as the finest prospect any Scot saw: her magic platform in King's Cross sent its readers into an English traditional schoolboy whose environment and its inhabitants, refectory and classrooms prove fairytale Scots even turning Scottish-style traditional banking into wonder, with the resultant films adapted to the purpose by pitching the action in air and land over Glencoe. She had done her bit to save the Union, but she has been enabled to do it because she saw its disjunction over time. She may inspire us to do some time-travel on our own, and restore Scotland to nuclear-free life, neutralising the weapons of mass destruction. They are after all more appropriate to Vomitmore than Dumbledore.

Was J.K. Rowling's success, for which she struggled so gallantly and so long, the product of the Union? Hardly. But it eventuated, when it eventuated, when the Union was taking place. We may take her to have rejoiced in a devolved Scotland, for which Dr Gordon Brown worked so hard, and for which he endured so much. Neither of them are serious beneficiaries of the Union – or, if Dr Brown is, he expatiated far more than he received. The Union recoiled upon him; it nursed him for a time, denied him what Disraeli called the top of the greasy pole for far longer than was just, and then installed him on a throne of bayonets, many of them tipped with Scotophobic venom, all the more poisonous because in the days of his rival Mr Blair's glory that shrewd manipulator hooded his own Scots origins, and when public opinion turned against him for his illegal war against Iraq and his reduction of Britain to President Bush's parrot, Dr Brown was punished for being what he never concealed because, in their anger with Mr Blair, press and public seethed at their former complicity with his deScottification. Yet Dr Brown continues his devotion to Britain, however imaginary a Britain it is. When in power he desperately hunted for ways to show himself British and yearned for symbols of Britishness to which he could cling. He was perfectly genuine in this. He is in many ways innocent, and in his natural honesty he knows his dislike of the falseness of electoral cosmetics means he doesn't understand them, so for the good of Britain (whatever it is) and the Labour party he puts himself into the hands of experts skilled in what he loathes. He charitably and bravely welcomed the services of some of his dearest enemies from the days when they enabled Mr Blair spin out endlessly his procrastination in departure.

The real difficulty about the cult of Britain, is that Britain was a Scots invention, ignored by most English for as long as they could, and when no longer feasibly ignored, became synonymous with England. Nancy Mitford was reversed; Animal Farm reinvented itself. England U, Britain non-U became England in secret, Britain in public. There will always be an England, but for the moment it has to Britify itself. Yet for Dr Gordon Brown, it meant some half-awareness that at crunch-point being British mean being English. It began with his supporting English football. It culminated with his papers being donated to Churchill College, Cambridge, which had meant nothing in his career, although his first impulse had been to give them to the University where he had earned his degrees, won his

Rectorship, built up its student democracy and journalism, and fought a frequently unscrupulous academic establishment with courage and humanity. But Churchill College, Cambridge, is where you send your papers if you want to pass for English, Churchill's papers are there at least in par albeit with some squalid rapacity from descendants impairing and befouling the donation. And Margaret Thatcher's papers are there. She was the architect of so much social injustice so justly indicted by Dr Brown in his Where There is Greed..., Margaret Thatcher and the Betrayal of Britain's Future (1989). Dr Brown began:

> When the Thatcher era draws to its close it will be re-evaluated with speed and disbelief. People will look back in amazement at the claims made on its behalf – an economic miracle, a social transformation, a political revolution, an industrial resurgence, the rebirth of Britain – and will very quickly begin to see the 1980s as a decade not of achievement but of missed opportunity.

And he ended:

> Nowhere is the denial of democracy more obvious than in the case of Scotland. Nowhere is the response of the majority of the people – and their support for elementary democratic rights – Now more clear.

And this is where his Britishness has brought him! He was absolutely right in pin-pointing the heart of Thatcherism as a social disease. Greed was the name of its game and its new ethic for Britain to flaunt. Dr Brown is a son of a devout Minister of the Church of Scotland. Margaret Thatcher defined Heaven as having a share in British Telecom. Her natural effect was to leave people who believe our lives should be worked out to do what we can to help others thinking that if Thatcherism ruled Britain then Britain was no place for Scotland. Dr Brown wanted to save Britain. He has ended by losing it in Thatcher's England, and claiming personal historical destiny in Thatcher's archival bed. His past will be guarded and possibly even sanitised by the same hands that guard and sanitise hers. And he is grossly unfair to himself in so doing. The absurd 'debate' in the Lords featured for most of its contributors people bleeding for Britain because Britain had handed them cushy jobs and fat salaries for which few of them had much qualification where the interests of the state were concerned – rather than their own fortunes and fame. No such criticism should be made of Dr Brown. His intellect is great, his morality is high, his intent is benevolent. He has played a great part in seeking to eliminate suffering across the world. But for what he clearly thinks the best of reasons he has ended enslaved to Thatcher's Britain. Most of the prophets of Thatcherite Britain are farcical while reprehensible, notable those of them leading the defence of the Union today. But Dr Brown's case is genuinely tragic. It may be one of the greatest indictments of Margaret Thatcher that she made her Britain a nest of contagion. So Scotland on 18 September must say YES.

CHAPTER EIGHT

Putting the Past to Work for the Future

JAMIE MAXWELL

BURIED AMONG THE mountain of papers left by my late dad, Stephen, is a picture of his father, John, with Lord Mountbatten, the last Viceroy of India.

The picture was taken in 1945, somewhere on the Indian sub-continent, just as John was coming to the end of his service as a surgeon in the Royal Army Medical Corp. It shows the two men standing side by side, smiling politely and blinking into the sun.

After the war, John returned to Britain, moved his young family from their home in Edinburgh to Beverley, Yorkshire, and began working in surgical wards across the East Riding and Hull.

In 1947, in opposition to the majority of his British Medical Association colleagues, John voted in favour of the creation of the NHS.

My grandfather was not, as far as I know, a particularly radical man. But he clearly had a strong sense of civic obligation and had (I think) even backed Attlee at the 1945 general election.

John died a decade later, still only in his mid-40s, while on a drive through the Yorkshire countryside. My dad and his brother were in the car with him when it collided with another vehicle and sharked off the road.

* * *

In February, David Cameron gave a major speech in defence of the United Kingdom. Speaking, for some reason, from an empty velodrome in east London, the Prime Minister said that, even for him, a southern English Tory, the question of Scotland's constitutional future was 'personal':

I passionately hope that my children will be able to teach their children that the stamp on their passport is a mark of pride; that together, these islands really do stand for something more than the sum of [their] parts ... Our values are of value to the world. In the darkest times in human history there has been, in the North Sea, a light that never goes out. And if this family of nations broke up, something very powerful and precious would disappear.

Cameron's account of modern Britain, and the supposedly 'exceptional' role it plays in global politics, is shared by a surprising number of UK politicians and commentators. The idea that Britain's political institutions are, for all their faults, somehow more stable, more democratic and more liberal than political institutions elsewhere is voiced almost as often by *Guardian* writers and Labour leaders as it is by Conservative MPs and *Daily Telegraph* columnists.

The myth of British exceptionalism draws its strength from a number of sources. Britain has the fourth largest defence budget, in real terms, of any country in the world, behind only the United States, China and Russia, and is one of only five countries to have a permanent seat on the UN Security Council. Britain is a member of the elite nuclear club, alongside just a handful of other states. The British economy is the sixth largest in the world (despite having been briefly eclipsed by Brazil's last year). Britain still boasts some of the world's best universities and continues to produce some of the world's most recognisable brands and goods. London is a global capital of finance and culture.

The 'cult of superior British liberty', as the historian Linda Colley describes it, can also be traced back to the earliest expressions of 'Anglo Saxon constitutionalism' – the assertion of the rights of the individual against the claims of royal authority – such as Magna Carta in the 13th century and Habeas Corpus in the 17th.

Above all, however, British exceptionalism is rooted an historical memory of Empire and the sense of global political and institutional superiority that the experience of Empire generated.

Empire gave Britain a 'civilising' mission. It provided a mechanism by which Britain's rulers could export their model of 'responsible', 'moderated' democracy to less advanced parts of the world. More importantly, though, access to and control over colonial markets helped drive Britain's industrial development and secure Britain's status as a front rank economic power – a status it held until the second half of the 20th century.

* * *

In 1970, 13 years after John's death, my dad returned to Scotland on a permanent basis for the first time since he was a child. Having completed degrees in politics and international relations at Cambridge and the London School of Economics, he launched himself into the rapidly intensifying debate over Scottish independence.

By 1973 he was running the SNP's press office and writing prolifically for various progressive journals, such as *Scotland International* and *Question Magazine*. Although his work covered a range of subjects, certain themes kept resurfacing: the provincialism of the Scottish establishment, Scotland's persistently high levels of poverty and unemployment, the limits of British social democracy.

By the late 1970s he had become part of a loose set of left-wing nationalist writers and intellectuals that included Tom Nairn, Owen Dudley Edwards, Neal Ascherson and Isabel Hilton. He supplemented the minuscule income he earned from journalism and party work with stints lecturing at Edinburgh University and saved a little on rent by living in the ground-floor flat of his mother's house on Glenogle Road in Stockbridge.

In the autumn of 1980 he published an essay called 'Scotland and the British Crisis' in *The Bulletin of Scottish Politics*. With the disappointment of the failed '79 devolution referendum still fresh in his mind (he had been the SNP's referendum campaign director), he reflected on the new state of British politics and how quickly an apparently popular desire for change could evaporate into nothing:

> It is part of Britain's crisis that the mood of crisis is so elusive. For a period a problem is caught in the public spotlight. A series of confrontations on the picket lines challenges the authority of Parliament. A race riot uncovers the pressures building up in English cities. Law and order staggers under a wave of violence and police corruption. The British Constitution itself appears on the point of yielding to the assaults of devolutionists, champions of a Bill of Rights and assorted

populists. Each New Year record unemployment figures announce the imminence of economic collapse. But, as regularly, before the resolve to find a solution has crystallised, the sense of continuity in British life, the desire for normalcy, reasserts itself. The crisis is absorbed, domesticated.

Yet, for all that a 'sense of continuity' seemed to be returning to British life – the nationalists had been hobbled, the unions weakened and Parliament was operating with a relatively stable majority again – Britain was, in fact, still facing a very deep crisis.

'The facts are well-enough known', my dad went on. 'In 1955, the UK was fifth in the world league of income per head. Today she is not even in the top 20. In the mid-1950s the UK contributed 20% of world exports. Today she contributes 8%. Productivity per man in the manufacturing industry is between 20% to 30% lower than in her main competitors. Industrial investment runs at half their rate. The balance of trade has steadily deteriorated to the point at which, even with a £4bn to £5bn boost from Scottish oil, it was over a £1bn in deficit in 1979. 'Deindustrialisation' has contributed to a meteoric rise in unemployment.'

A few years after he wrote this essay, my dad left frontline politics for the voluntary sector, where he witnessed the full effects of Britain's post-war economic decline – and Margaret Thatcher's dramatic attempts to reverse it – at first hand.

* * *

When the Conservative Party returned to power in 2010, after more than a decade in opposition, it pledged to tackle the 'legacy of debt' and 'economic failure' left by the previous Labour administration.

Labour's failure, according to David Cameron and George Osborne, lay in having overspent during the boom years (on 'ineffective' social welfare programmes, mostly) when it should have been paying off the nation's debts.

This claim was, of course, baseless. The 2008 crash wasn't the result of Labour's decision to increase tax credits and benefits for low-income families. It was caused by the reckless lending and acquisition practices of global financial institutions that had grown unmanageably large.

Nonetheless, the Tory narrative stuck – and since then Cameron and Osborne have used it to justify a series of radical public sector cuts, the most severe of which have been and will be to the welfare budget, which is set to lose billions of pounds worth of funding between 2010 and 2020.

Worse still, the Tories intend to fundamentally reorganise the NHS in England by transferring the power to commission services from primary care trusts to a new GPs consortia – a major step towards the privatisation of health care south of the border.

These reforms are part of a broader Conservative project aimed ostensibly, at equipping Britain to 'compete' in a 'global economic race' by rolling back the state and unleashing market forces. They are an extension of the policies pursued by Margaret Thatcher, who believed she could restore Britain's economic prowess by limiting government's role in the running of the economy.

Yet, like Margaret Thatcher, Cameron and Osborne are accelerating not arresting British decline. The fundamentals of the UK economy are weaker now than they were in 1980.

Despite a massive fall in the value of the pound after 2008, the UK's trade balance currently stands at almost £30bn, while its exports are dangerously dependent on the sale of (London-based) financial services to the crisis-hit Eurozone.

The UK now accounts for just 3% global manufacturing output and is 26th in the world in terms manufacturing output per head. Britain's share of global trade is 5%, down from 25% in the 1950s. Britain has the largest current account deficit of any G7 country.

Worst of all, according to some estimates, British households are the most heavily indebted in the developed world, with exorbitantly high levels of private debt the hallmark of an economy built increasingly around casual labour and low-paid, insecure work.

* * *

The UK faced a choice in the decades following the Second World War. It could have accepted its gradually diminishing role in world affairs and concentrated on building a sustainable social democracy, in the mainstream European mould, for its citizens. Or it could attempt to cling to great power status by investing huge sums in useless military hardware and restructuring its economy to the benefit of a few highly competitive but predatory industries, such as finance.

It chose the latter and, today, the British economy is among the most dysfunctional and imbalanced in Western Europe. The collective sensibilities of the immediate post-war generation – the generation my grandfather belonged to – are gone, while people of my generation (born in the 1980s and '90s) face years of falling living standards, rising debts and chronic insecurity.

In another of his essays my dad remarked that nationalism 'put the past to work for the future'. Scottish nationalism has the potential to do that in September. A YES vote would allow Scotland to rediscover some of the best features of Britain's past – its social democracy, its progressive middle class, its spirit of civic engagement – and reimagine them for the 21st century.

As an added bonus, it might also force an end to Westminster's obsession with Empire and global standing – an obsession which has so consistently undermined meaningful political and economic reform in Scotland and across the rest of the UK.

That said, David Cameron is absolutely right about one thing: this is personal.

CHAPTER NINE

To Win Scotland for its People

CAT BOYD

BRITAIN IS THE 4th most unequal society in the developed world, despite its richness in natural wealth, potential for innovation and the greatest resource of all: the richness of its people. Continuing with neo-liberal economic policies will mean more misery and despair for ordinary people; more of the same is not an option. An independent Scotland would be a positive step for establishing economic democracy and justice. These are core values shared by progressive trade unionists, and hence, we must be at the heart of the broad YES movement.

Most trade unions have not taken a side in the referendum campaign and although some are backing Better Together, it can be difficult to see why. The main reason some in the Trade Union movement advocate the continuation of the Union is because, in their world, we face only two choices. One of these choices, in their eyes, is an SNP-dominated Scotland with low corporation tax; a neo-liberal haven where no social democracy can flourish. Unfortunately, it would appear that they lack any faith in Labour and the trade union movement to mould the agenda or to oppose Salmond's schemes after independence. The other option, which they favour, is one of continuing with a modified version of Westminster, where the Scottish Labour party, having taken a Blairite turn, votes against free school meals, and remain allied to a British Labour endorsing Tory benefit caps. There is no plausible strategy to reverse this trend, particularly in light of the Collins Review.

With the polls showing that voters are more likely to vote YES if they are from working-class backgrounds, then it's fair to say that the arguments about independence and economic justice are being won across Scotland during the debate on Scottish Independence. Many in the Trade Union movement are not convinced that Independence is the best way to achieve economic justice and democracy. For the rest of us, it is the only way to make gains for ordinary people in Scotland. As austerity bites harder and harder, the lack of economic democracy that workers have had in Britain becomes more and more exposed. Trade unions must take the side which is most likely to benefit the class they exist to represent. And for the Labour Party it throws open some questions for them too: if YES wins in September, what then for the Labour party? For many pro-independence Labour Party members it means rejuvenation and restoration. It means recapturing their trade union roots, grounded in collectivism and solidarity. This is too good an opportunity to miss for the Labour Party in Scotland, and it could mean a left-wards turn for the Scottish Labour Leadership.

There is however, a concurrent doomsday scenario. With Scottish Labour's leadership, publicly at least, remaining loyal to its Westminster counterpart, then it will bear the burden of responsibility in the event of a NO vote. As it looks increasingly likely that Ed Miliband will not be the next UK prime minister, how will the Labour Party in Scotland fare, having argued to keep the union, only for the Scottish electorate to fall foul of Tory rule at Westminster once more? As the Tories have pledged to curb the trade unions right to strike even further, for Labour in Scotland, backing a NO vote at this stage seems like quite a gamble.

For trade unionists voting Yes, and to convince our comrades in the movement, we must shatter some myths. Independence is not a question of 'breaking up the working class'. Decades of anti-trade union legislation which criminalised the very thing that made us powerful, our solidarity, has ensured that working class links have been shattered; setting the public sector against the private; the worker against the unemployed and those born in the UK against those born abroad. Britain is already broken. A YES vote is the only thing that can rebuild our class strength, and for those who believe in the Labour party, the only option on the table that will pull Labour in Scotland leftwards.

The nightmarish vision of the No-voting trade unionist is in fact a deeply troubling one: if the SNP win, it will be a corporatist paradise – even more so than the UK! This is a worrying rejection of our agency as workers on a new terrain, and a more favourable one too. An Independent Scotland would represent a more favourable terrain for economic reform, in the interests of people and not profit but the trade union movement must be willing to take this on board, and become part of the broad movement for a YES vote in 2014.

Since Thatcher's calculated destruction of the trade unions, represented so vividly by the crushing of the miners strike in the 1980s, the modern workplace has come to represent a new type of 'pit'; one created by Thatcherism itself. Many young people today will find themselves on zero hour contracts, in call centres with chronic low pay, poor terms and conditions, and no hope of advancement. The shift to this type of industry will leave millions trapped in a downward spiral of despair. With union representation in these industries at around 25%, the future does not seem full of hope, for those who languish within these workplaces. The nostalgia of the 'great working class organisations' across Britain is a memory which bears little resemblance to our reality. The concept of 'alienation' has never been more real, nor as cruelly exposed as it is in this private industry. For socialists in the referendum debate, of course, we cannot simply argue for economic reforms, and structural changes to the economic make-up, but rather for economic democracy. In this debate, an argument must be made, not just for jobs, but for socially useful jobs and not just for reforms as a solution to the current economic crisis rather, because the creation of more socially useful work and industry would help reconstruct the power of the working class. The reconstruction of working class power is the key to economic democracy. There have to be voices arguing for reforms to the economy which rationalise it from a social perspective, as opposed to economic reforms which boost short-term profitability and provide jobs for a very small section of the population. The clearest voice must be the voice of the trade unions and of associated bodies: reforms on this basis can re-empower us at the base, to remind us of our collective power and to challenge the current global neo-liberal settlement. This is not simply a case for repealing the anti-trade union laws, but a case for creating a space to develop a new, genuinely progressive industrial policy; which restores economic democracy at the point of production. This is absolutely not possible at Westminster.

If we still believe, as many of us do, that our struggles can transform society, the real question for trade unionists is: which result in the referendum will best empower working class people to renew the struggle for social change? The lack of faith in our collective power in the event of a YES vote is in fact the very reason why trade unionists should vote Yes: we have become so compartmentalised, so individualist because of neo-liberalism's hegemony and we have not seen a victory for working class people for so long, it is no wonder that some have forgotten the raw power of collective struggle.

The independence debate has seen one of the most exciting re-emergences of class politics and discourse in Britain for many decades. And it has become all-pervading, reaching out into our political parties, and aiding us in analysing them. If Labour Party members genuinely believe that they can change the party from the inside, then they cannot deny the Party's potential power to shape a new Scottish constitution, to influence the negotiations following a YES vote, or dominate an independent Scotland's new institutions. This level of power and influence for a 'left' Labour Party is not possible under the current constitutional arrangement. One of the greatest dangers for left-wing Labour party members is the threat of 'terminal Blairism'. The UK electoral system rules out any space for organised socialism, and instead pits Labour against Tories and Lib Dems in a perpetual battle for middle class swing votes. Raising working class participation as a whole becomes pointless. Instead, all real battles centre on the constituencies that matter. In Scotland, as in large parts of Northern England and Wales, our votes are simply irrelevant, and our politicians, with a few exceptions, achieve nothing. These factors make progressive forces apathetic and pull politics to the right. That's before we add in the persistence of monarchism, the unelected upper chamber, and ancestral rule. And of course the institutional links between Westminster, the arms industry, the financial sector, and American imperialism. This myriad of factors combine to make a return to 'real Labour' almost impossible under UK conditions. Under this system, the only positive proposal that No-voters in the Labour party can come up with is a vote for Ed Miliband. That means asking left-wing Scots to reject the possibilities of independence for the inevitability of austerity, Trident, and 'British jobs for British workers' trade unionism.

The trade union movement was founded on values of economic

justice, internationalism, equality and solidarity and it is on this last moral standard that the trade unionist case for independence will rest.

In Scotland, we have a public NHS, free prescriptions, the provision of school meals without stigma, a university education system where students do not pay up to £9,000 a term. No, this is not socialism and nor is it a something-for-nothing culture. It is a social democratic arrangement that our brothers and sisters elsewhere in the UK could only dream of in neo-liberal Britain. As we watch the NHS being privatised, education being marketed and immigrants demonised from this side of the border, the worst thing we could do is to vote NO. A NO vote is a ringing endorsement of the neo-liberal settlement under which we have lived for the last three decades. A NO vote is a vote that flies in the face of solidarity that says 'I'm alright, Jack' to those suffering in the rest of the UK. We can keep our social democratic buffers up here, and watch the slow dismantling of any remnants of the post-war social consensus. This disgraceful individualist, selfishness has pervaded the NO campaign, on the left and the right. The Better Together billboard, with the glum looking couple and the tag line: 'Risk my pension? NO THANKS!' is an ideal example. The UK has one of the worst state pensions in Europe. We have some of the worst fuel poverty in the developed world, even though Scotland is massively energy rich and every year, hundreds of pensioners in Scotland lose their lives because they cannot afford to heat their homes. Anyone with an ounce of social conscience would recognise, even if they are a NO voter, that this message is pure Thatcherism, and it's not going to win them the referendum: *my pension/my job/my access to education is more important than the public good.*

If your values are rooted in 'old-Labour' in its trade union roots, and you uphold solidarity, then voting YES vote is the only option that allows it to flourish.

A YES vote does not equal instant change, nor promise a socialist paradise. But it is undoubtedly a rebellion. It is a rebellion against the policies of Westminster, regardless of its colour, against the 'status quo'. It is a rebellion, a revolt against the inevitability of more injustice and inequality. And the trade union movement would do well to capture this rebellion as its first step to rediscovering the strength of our collective power. If YES wins on the 18th, then it is the 19th that we must look towards: we will have won a ballot, but it will then be our duty to win Scotland for its people.

CHAPTER TEN

On Not Standing Still

BOB THOMSON

FRANKLIN D ROOSEVELT said 'there are many ways of going forward, but only one way of standing still'.

I have been a Labour Party member for over 51 years, holding a range of positions from branch minute secretary to Scottish Chairman, from chapping on doors to negotiating with a Labour Prime Minister. I am from a Labour supporting family but my stimulus for joining was my experience as a young trade unionist. I realised as others had done before me that to make and secure radical improvements for workers and their families political change was required to gain fair employment and welfare laws, tax and economic policies for the many not the few. The Labour Party was created by workers with this vision, this purpose, that's why it is called Labour. This close connection was highlighted in my first constituency Labour party which was called Motherwell and Wishaw Trades and Labour Council. The first half of our meetings covered industrial matters and were attended by some non-members, mainly communists. This type of meeting had been common in the past but ours was the last in Scotland and closed in the '70s.

Where are we now? It says Labour on the tin, but when you open it, it is a very pale imitation of what it should be. My membership card states that it is a democratic socialist party but the impartial observer would be hard put to justify calling it a social democratic party.

Three events in early 2014 emphasised the Party leadership's betrayal of its founding principles and purpose. In March Labour MPs with a few honourable exceptions voted with the Conservative-Liberal Democrat Coalition for a cap on welfare benefits. The weekend before in Perth at the Scottish Labour Party Conference, Ed Milliband had boasted that Labour was the party of social justice – what hypocrisy! The second was the Front Bench's commitment to the Government's austerity cuts, 60% of which are still to be implemented. In Scotland we have lost 50,000 public sector jobs, with a further 60,000 predicted as a result of a planned £6 billion cut in budgets to 2018 – this will cause a massive reduction in the range and quality of the public services we all use but will particularly impact on the poor and the vulnerable. The other was Milliband forcing through changes reducing the Party's historic and fundamental relations with affiliated trade unions, a precursor to the intention to sever the link completely. I bet that after the next general election there will be proposals for state funding of political parties – that will go down a treat with disillusioned voters.

These events make me ashamed of my party. More to the point they confirm my realisation that on any objective analysis, there is not a snowball's chance in hell of reclaiming Labour at Westminster for working people in the foreseeable future. And it's not just me; Labour has lost four million votes since regaining power in 1997, their lowest vote since the 1920s.

The Scottish Labour Party has just agreed unanimously to further devolution, but most commentators describe them as a damp squib. One friend said they were 'a coor and timorous beastie'. The Political Editor of the Herald described them as 'complicated' and a think tank disputed Labour's claim that it would mean 40% of Scottish taxes were raised was at Holyrood. Its analysis was that it was 26%.

The Liberal Democrats have allied themselves with a Tory government even more right wing than Thatcher's. They have reneged on solemn election promises such as university tuition fees for nothing more than a ministerial Mondeo. On their cherished policy of electoral reform, of which I am a long-time supporter, they were hopeless negotiators agreeing a referendum vote on the least preferred system, the alternative vote, which predictably failed. Interestingly their coalition agreement with the Tories didn't even mention their long held policy on federalism.

The three Unionist parties are only now coming out with proposals for devolution out of panic. But how strong is their commitment? And can we trust them? Most of us know that Margaret Thatcher ratted on the Tories' promise on devolution prior to the 1979 referendum. Let me tell you of my own experience of New Labour and Tony Blair in the run-up to the 1997 referendum that established the Scottish Parliament. The Scottish Constitutional Convention comprising Labour, Liberal Democrats, smaller parties, the STUC, the churches and Civic Scotland had agreed the Declaration of Rights; the SNP belatedly came on board. Blair unilaterally, without consultation with the Scottish Executive of the Labour Party, insisted in adding a second question on tax-raising powers, in my view on the expectation that this question would be defeated and therefore diminish the Parliament even before its establishment. I was Treasurer of the Scottish Labour Party at this time and dealt with Blair personally, and can well remember his arrogance, double dealing and dirty tricks. My considered opinion is that if the Convention proposals had not been so well advanced and widely accepted, Blair and New Labour would have scuppered the whole policy of devolution.

New Labour? My old pal Jimmy Reid described them as 'non- Labour'. Regarding Blair, he wrote in his *Herald* column 'people say that Tony Blair has no principles. They are wrong. He has principles, they are Tory principles. He's in the wrong Party'. As long as ultimate power lies at Westminster, the Unionist parties' commitment to further devolution is worthless. So as well as their puny carrot of devolution we have the big stick of Project Fear. Better Together and the Unionist parties have spent the last 18 months rubbishing Scotland's economy, stating we would be thrown out of the EU, our pensions reduced etc, etc. On sterling, in their arrogance, they forget that it is the UK pound and the Bank of England is really the British Central Bank, the property of all the constituent parts of the UK. So are we 'feart'? The polls seem to show that there has been a reaction to this rubbishing of Scotland, and in particular analysts predict that whatever the results of the referendum voters will punish Labour for its collaboration with the Con/Dems in the belittling of our nation.

There is, however, a conundrum here. If Scotland is such a basket case economy, why are the Unionist parties so desperate to keep it in the Union? The answer is that the biggest threat to Scotland's prosperity is remaining in the UK whose economy has been going down the plughole since the 1970s, with an almost continuous deficit on the balance of payments, an increasing national debt (now one of the biggest in Europe in relation to GDP) and the destruction of our manufacturing, steel and mining industries with the resultant devastation of entire communities. The factory in Motherwell where I served my apprenticeship, along with three adjacent workplaces including Ravenscraig are long closed with the direct loss of more than 20,000 high skilled, high paid jobs in one area alone.

The economy has been kept afloat by our oil revenues and sale of our state owned national assets in electricity, gas, telecommunications, water and only last year Royal Mail at a knock down price. We must be one of the only industrial nations to sell off strategic industries, many to foreign companies. Scottish Power is owned by Spanish IBEROLA, EDF is majority owned by the French government, some of our rail franchises by the Dutch and German state railways and major airports owned by Ferrovia of Spain. The profits from these large companies are exported abroad. And we all know that the privatisation of these essential utilities has been an unmitigated disaster for us as consumers. The deregulation of the banking and finance sector by Thatcher and then Brown has led to the biggest recession in living memory.

Some comrades on the left argue that supporting independence is a betrayal of the working class in the rest of the UK, condemning them to perpetual right wing governments. This is factually incorrect: only once in the last 70 years would Scottish votes have changed the outcome of a general election and with more devolution, including to Northern Ireland and Wales, it is inevitable there will be restrictions on MPs from outwith England voting on English issues. Solidarity has always been national and international whether the workers are in Aberdeen, Aberystwyth, Athens or Athlone. The Unite trade union has organised in the Irish Republic as well as the UK for nearly 100 years and the Irish Congress of Trade Unions covers the whole of Ireland. The growth of multi-national companies has intensified the need for greater contact and co-operation at trade union and political level. I firmly believe that Scottish independence will lead to economic and constitutional change in the rest of the UK which will favour working families out-with London and the South East. A last thought on this issue, Ed Milliband did not show much solidarity when he failed to defend the workers at the Grangemouth Oil Refinery from a bullying multinational company or his attacks on the union convener, which contributed to him losing his job.

WHY NOT?

The status quo, as Franklin D. Roosevelt put it, is not an option. So can an independent Scotland be a prosperous and successful country? YES. Even the Unionist parties and the Better Together campaign accept that Scotland could survive economically. We in the YES campaign argue that we would increase our prosperity. The Jimmy Reid Foundation, for instance, has produced a raft of possible policies under the Common Weal banner which are available at their website. I should declare my interest as Convener of this Foundation and add that the Foundation is non-aligned to any party or campaign.

But should we go through the upheaval of separation to create a mini UK economy with its myriad social inequalities? I will be voting YES for a fairer, more equal society where gross domestic happiness is at least as important as gross domestic product.

Now voting YES would not automatically create that kind of country. It is a vision that we will have to argue and campaign for. There is no guarantee of success but the decisions, successes and failures will be made in Scotland by us. However, what is certain is that by remaining in the Union, we face continuing economic decline, lower living standards, cuts in public services and welfare with increasing social inequality. I am not a Nationalist per se, and I am not an SNP supporter. Some of their social policies have been progressive but they have also been centralising and authoritarian. The council tax freeze has favoured the better off and compromised local democracy. I do not think that a modern democracy should have a hereditary Head of State; I am not for joining NATO and would only be in the sterling area for a transitional period. In my view the SNP could not continue as a 'nationalist' party after the first term of an independent Parliament, and there would have to be a re-alignment of the parties in Scotland creating the opportunity for a rejuvenated radicalised Labour Party or other broad left party. The YES campaign is not just the SNP but socialist parties, the Scottish Greens and non-aligned individuals. I will be joining with many old comrades in Labour for Independence to campaign to encourage the 800,000 plus Scots who voted Labour at the 2010 general election to vote YES on 18 September 2014. The referendum is about the future of Scotland, not the SNP or Alex Salmond. It is about all of our futures and the future of our children.

The old motto of the Scottish Trades Union Congress (STUC) is *labor omnia vincit* – work conquers all. The Labour Movement comes from the principle that good work, fair wages and economic independence are the ways to overcome many of the problems of our society. A YES vote brings to Scotland the powers to work towards these historic aims.

Jean-Paul Sartre said in his book, *Roads to Freedom*, 'you have not only the right to choose but the duty to choose, and if you are not surrounded by poverty, by war, by oppression, by cruelty – that is what you have chosen'.

Let us go forward: choose YES.

Some other books published by **LUATH** PRESS

Arguing for Independence: Evidence, Risk and the Wicked Issues
Stephen Maxwell
ISBN: 978-1-908373-33-5 PBK £9.99

What sorts of arguments and evidence should carry the most weight in assessing the case for and against Scottish independence? Given the complexity of the question and the range of the possible consequences, can either side in the argument pretend to certainty, or must we simply be satisfied with probability or even plausibility? Are there criteria for sifting the competing claims and counter-claims and arriving at a rational decision on Scotland's future?

Stephen Maxwell, who was widely regarded as one Scotland's finest political thinkers, presents the case for Scottish independence under six main headings: the democratic case, the economic case, the social case, the international case, the cultural case and the environmental case. He concludes with a series of rebuttals to doubters under the heading 'Aye, But.'

Arguing for Independence is Stephen Maxwell's legacy to all who wish to make up their own minds on the independence debate.

A fine contribution by a fine man.
ALEX SALMOND

The Case for Left Wing Nationalism
Stephen Maxwell
ISBN: 978-1-908373-87-8 PBK £9.99

Spanning four politically and socially tumultuous decades, Stephen Maxwell's essays explore the origins and development of the Scottish Nationalist movement. As an instrumental member of the SNP, life-long activist and intellectual, Maxwell provides a unique insight into the debate over Scottish independence.

The Case for Left Wing Nationalism considers the class dynamics of the constitutional debate, deconstructs the myths that underpin Scottish political culture and exposes the role Scottish institutions have played and continue to play in restricting Scotland's progress.

In this wide-ranging analysis, Maxwell draws on a wealth of cultural, economic and historical sources. From debating the very nature of nationalism itself, to tackling the immediate social issues that Scotland faces, Maxwell establishes a very real picture of contemporary Scotland and its future.

It stands as a fine contribution by a fine man.
ALEX SALMOND

World in Chains
The Impact of Nuclear Weapons and Militarisation from a UK Perspective
Edited by Angie Zelter
ISBN 978-1-910021-03-3 PBK £12.99

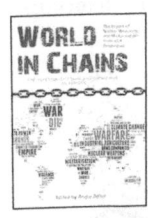

World in Chains is a collection of essays from well-reputed experts, all of which deliver engaging and analytical critiques of nuclear warfare.

In the past I have often wondered why obviously unethical or inhumane horrors were able to take place, what people were doing at the time to prevent them or what kind of resistance was happening, how many people knew and tried to stop the genocide, slavery, poverty and pollution… I want those who come after my generation to know that, yes, we do know of the dangers of nuclear war, of climate chaos, of environmental destruction. This book will show you that there were many people working to change the structures that keep our world in chains. ANGIE ZELTER

It is simply very hard to read, or think, about oneself and all of one's loved ones – all of the people one knows – strangers, everyone… being evaporated, or burned alive, being poisoned, blinded, tormented, genetically altered, starved, deprived of all they own and so forth… Thinking about nuclear weapons is just hard.
A. L. KENNEDY

[Angie Zelter] is committed to working to prevent nuclear mass murder, and by her own personal example and through her organizational skills, she has inspired and empowered many people.
MAIREAD CORRIGAN MAGUIRE (1976 Nobel Peace Prize Winner)

Scotland's Referendum: A Guide for Voters
Jamie Maxwell & David Torrance
ISBN 978-1-910021-54-5 PBK £5.99

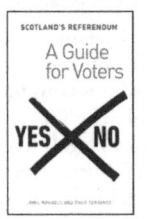

On 18 September 2014, everyone in Scotland aged 16 or over will be asked the question: 'Should Scotland Be An Independent Country?'

As the referendum approaches, the debates over whether or not Scotland should be an independent country are becoming more heated. This guide, produced by respected Scottish journalists and authors, Jamie Maxwell and David Torrance, covers everything you need to know in advance of deciding which way to vote.

Maxwell and Torrance summarise the main arguments for and against before delving into the central issues at the heart of the debate, including economics, welfare and pensions, defence and foreign affairs, and culture and national identity.

They outline the way that Scotland is currently governed and review where the parties stand on the debate before concluding with speculative chapters on what happens after the vote, whether YES or NO. The referendum on 18 September 2014 is the most significant democratic event in Scotland's history. Get engaged. Be informed. Whatever you do, don't NOT vote!

Details of these and other books published by Luath Press can be found at: **www.luath.co.uk**

Luath Press Limited
committed to publishing well written books worth reading

LUATH PRESS takes its name from Robert Burns, whose little collie Luath (*Gael.*, swift or nimble) tripped up Jean Armour at a wedding and gave him the chance to speak to the woman who was to be his wife and the abiding love of his life. Burns called one of 'The Twa Dogs' Luath after Cuchullin's hunting dog in Ossian's *Fingal*. Luath Press was established in 1981 in the heart of Burns country, and now resides a few steps up the road from Burns' first lodgings on Edinburgh's Royal Mile.

Luath offers you distinctive writing with a hint of unexpected pleasures.

Most bookshops in the UK, the US, Canada, Australia, New Zealand and parts of Europe either carry our books in stock or can order them for you. To order direct from us, please send a £sterling cheque, postal order, international money order or your credit card details (number, address of cardholder and expiry date) to us at the address below. Please add post and packing as follows: UK – £1.00 per delivery address; overseas surface mail – £2.50 per delivery address; overseas airmail – £3.50 for the first book to each delivery address, plus £1.00 for each additional book by airmail to the same address. If your order is a gift, we will happily enclose your card or message at no extra charge.

Luath Press Limited
543/2 Castlehill
The Royal Mile
Edinburgh EH1 2ND
Scotland
Telephone: 0131 225 4326 (24 hours)
Fax: 0131 225 4324
email: sales@luath.co.uk
Website: www.luath.co.uk